UNBOTS UNMASKED

Exposing cyberfraud in the era of AI

BENJAMIN FABRE

Bots Unmasked: Exposing Cyberfraud in the Era of AI

ISBN-13: 979-8-218-61346-4

Cover design by Alexis Rabeuf

Interior layout by John H. Matthews / johnhmatthews.com

TABLE OF CONTENTS

INTRODUCTION

Before I started detecting bots, I spent a decade developing them. At a social media monitoring venture, where I was part of the founding team, we built bots that were quite effective at navigating the web without being detected.

In fact, it was their very success that revealed a critical insight: if our "good" bots could navigate undetected, malicious ones could do the same—and on a massive scale. The tools we were refining to gather insights could just as easily be weaponized to attack websites, scrape data, and commit fraud. The traffic these bots generated was colossal, and their potential for harm was undeniable.

This realization led to a pivotal shift—the internet had a bot problem, and we had inadvertently been training for the job of solving it. Protecting the digital world from malicious bots became our mission.

Over the past decade, we've witnessed bots grow more sophisticated, from basic web scrapers to advanced entities leveraging headless browsers distributed on millions of clean residential IP addresses. These bots execute intricate tasks, evade detection, and wreak havoc across industries.

It's not just the volume of attacks that has surged, but their complexity and impact. What began as simple automated scripts has evolved into complex systems capable of mimicking human behavior with alarming precision, making it easier for fraudsters to take advantage of websites, mobile apps, and

APIs through various types of attacks. These range from account takeover to data theft, payment fraud to influence fraud, and more.

DataDome was created out of a necessity to address this escalating threat. The founding team realized that businesses of all sizes were increasingly vulnerable to bot-driven attacks that could compromise their operations, finances, reputations, and even their customers' PII and financial funds.

However, it's not all bad. With a strong fraud detection strategy, you can stop bots and protect your business and customers. Our journey at DataDome has been one of constant innovation, staying ahead of these evolving threats and ensuring our solutions are always one step ahead of the attackers.

This book encapsulates the insights and expertise we've gained through our fight against bots. It is designed to provide a comprehensive guide for businesses to understand, detect, and mitigate bot-driven fraud.

We review the history and evolution of bots, exploring how they've transformed from rudimentary scripts into sophisticated tools of cybercrime. We detail the various types of bots and their mechanisms, the favored techniques used by fraudsters, and the far-reaching impacts of bots and fraud on different industries. We also look at the intersection of AI and bots, exploring how AI is being harnessed both by fraudsters and bot protection providers.

Through detailed case studies and industry-specific analyses, we illustrate the advanced methods employed by attackers and their impact on your business. Beyond knowledge, we offer practical, actionable tips on recognizing signs of bot infiltration and online fraud, and key considerations to protect your business.

At DataDome, we believe in the power of community and education in combating cyber threats. We hope it will inspire those who read it to share their experiences, and learn from one another. We are committed to fostering a collaborative environment where insights and strategies are openly exchanged, strengthening our defense together.

We also emphasize the importance of ongoing education. As threats evolve, so too must our knowledge and skills. This book provides a foundation, but staying ahead requires continuous learning and adaptation.

As we look to the future, I see a convergence of fraud and cybersecurity teams working together to tackle not just the bot issue but a broader spectrum of online threats. This collaboration will be crucial in developing comprehensive defense strategies and enhancing the ability to detect, analyze, and respond to various attacks and fraud. By sharing expertise, data, and resources, these teams can create a more resilient and proactive cybersecurity posture, better equipped to stop fraud before it happens.

By the end of this book, you will be equipped with the tools and knowledge necessary to protect your digital environments from the ever-present threat of bots and online fraud. Whether you are a business owner, IT professional, or cybersecurity expert, our insights will help guide you in making informed decisions that enhance your cybersecurity posture.

Let's work to eliminate cyberfraud, together.

Benjamin Fabre, CEO & Co-Founder of DataDome

CHAPTER 1: WHAT IS A BOT? THE GOOD, THE BAD, & THE UGLY

When us humans are faced with repetitive tasks, we often turn to automation to save time and avoid doing things manually. Bots—automated software programs—are designed precisely for that purpose. At its core, a bot is just a software application designed to automate a specific task, typically at a speed and scale far surpassing human capabilities.

However, like most tools, automation can be used for both good and bad. While many bots serve constructive purposes, like search engine crawlers and price comparison tools, others have been designed to cause harm and disruption.

Bots can be categorized primarily by the effect they have on the website's owners: have they been created to help the website or business in some way, or to harm it?

Good Bots: Enhancing Functionality

A good bot performs a helpful or useful task for your company or website visitors. Most of the time, it does not damage or worsen the user experience of the places it crawls.

A good bot is usually "good" because the website owner has a vested interest in it. It respects the webmaster's rules that regulate how often website bots should access the website. These rules are usually defined in the website's robots.txt file. A good bot should be programmed to look for that file, read it, and follow its rules before it does anything else.

Examples of good bots are:

- **Search engine bots**, such as Googlebot, Bingbot, the Baiduspider, YandexBot, and others. These bots crawl the vast World Wide Web to find the content that will improve search engine results.
- **Ads networks**, such as Google AdsBot, Taboola, or The Trade Desk. In order to offer optimized ad spaces, they research and analyze content and classify websites.
- **Social network bots**, such as Facebook Crawler and Pinterest Crawler. These bots crawl the websites that have been shared on social media networks to create better recommendations, fight spam, build a safer online environment, and more.
- **Marketing bots**, such as SEMrush bot, AhrefsBot, and Botify. All SEO and content marketing software platforms will use bots that crawl websites for backlinks, organic and paid keywords, traffic volume, and more.
- **Site monitoring bots**, such as Uptimebot, Pingdom, Datadog, and the PRTG Network Monitor. These bots ping your website to detect its overall performance and whether it's down or not.
- **Voice engine bots**, such as Alexa's Crawler and Applebot (Siri). Similar to search engine bots, these bots crawl the web so they can give accurate answers to the questions their users ask their voice assistant devices.

As you can see, many different types of good bots will want to crawl your website. This doesn't mean you should always let them, because good bots take up bandwidth too. For example, if you don't serve the Chinese or Russian markets, you may want to rate limit the Baiduspider and YandexBot.

It is also important to know that fraudsters often go out of their way to make their bots look like Googlebots. (DataDome spots more than one million hits per day coming from fake Googlebots on our customers' websites.) Googlebots should not be allowed based on their user agents alone, as they can easily be spoofed.

What is a Bad Bot?

A bad bot is a type of automated software programmed to perform tasks that can harm your company, your website visitors, or your operations. These tasks may include activities such as data theft, unauthorized content scraping, spam distribution, and other forms of malicious behavior.

Bad bots are typically deployed by individuals or groups with malicious intentions, aiming to disrupt services, steal sensitive information, or gain unfair advantages over competitors.

Bad bots vary significantly in their impact and legality. For example, scraping content from a website can be legal if done in compliance with the website's terms of service and relevant laws. However, when scraping is done excessively, aggressively, or without permission, it can degrade server performance, lead to data theft, and violate intellectual property rights. Whether a bot is considered harmful or acceptable therefore depends on the context and method of use.

Bad bots can be created and used by cybercriminals, fraudsters, unscrupulous competitors, or other malicious actors. They typically disregard the rules set out in the robots.txt file, which is intended to manage and restrict bot activity. Many of them also use sophisticated tools and frameworks to simulate human behavior and eschew detection.

Cyberattacks & Cyberfraud: The Dark Side of Bots

Beyond the "good" and the "bad" bots lies the ugly reality: bots are at the core of many cyber threats today. Their ability to automate complex actions makes bots indispensable tools for attackers, who can compromise a business's infrastructure and data security just as easily as they can commit fraud.

In fact, thanks to sophisticated bots, fraudsters can efficiently carry out activities such as card cracking, account takeover (ATO), and influence fraud, making bot attacks a leading cause of financial losses, reputational harm, and customer churn across industries.

Bots and Cybersecurity

Bots are essential tools for attackers seeking to exploit vulnerabilities, disrupt services, or gather sensitive information. One of the most significant risks is the use of bots to target a company's infrastructure, causing downtime, system breaches, or data theft.

Additionally, as businesses rely more heavily on APIs to power mobile apps, integrations, and online services, bots have become adept at abusing these interfaces, threatening data security and operational integrity.

Bot-Driven Fraud

> **"Bot mitigation is arguably the foundation of any fraud detection strategy designed to protect digital channels."**
>
> - Gartner, Market Guide for Online Fraud Detection, 12/22 (ID G00755906)

The financial, reputational, and compliance risks and costs associated with online fraud are enormous. Juniper Research forecasts cumulative merchant losses to online payment fraud globally between 2023 and 2027 to exceed $343 billion.[1] The US Federal Trade Commission (FTC) received more than 2.4 million fraud reports from consumers in 2022, a 30% increase from the previous year, with reported losses exceeding $8.8 billion.[2]

This impacts businesses in various ways:

- **Financial Losses**: Direct monetary losses from fraudulent transactions and the associated chargebacks.
- **Reputational Damage**: Loss of customer trust and brand value due to security breaches and fraudulent activities.
- **Compliance Costs**: Regulatory fines and increased costs associated with meeting compliance requirements after a data breach.

---

1 https://www.juniperresearch.com/press/online-payment-fraud-losses-to-exceed-343bn

2 https://www.ftc.gov/news-events/news/press-releases/2023/02/new-ftc-data-show-consumers-reported-losing-nearly-88-billion-scams-2022

Fraud can occur at every stage of the customer buying journey, from the homepage and product listings to account logins and the checkout process. This requires a comprehensive approach to detect and prevent fraudulent activities at all touchpoints.

In summary, bots are important tools for online fraudsters. They have become the primary enablers of many fraudulent activities, due to their ability to perform tasks at scale, faster, and more efficiently than humans.

To effectively combat online fraud, it is therefore crucial to shift focus from the downstream effects of fraud to the upstream drivers and attacks that enable it. This means stopping fraudsters at the metaphorical front door rather than at the vault door inside the bank.

CHAPTER 2: UNDERSTANDING THE THREAT LANDSCAPE

The ability to automate complex actions has made bots central to two primary threat areas: the cybersecurity threats that jeopardize infrastructure, systems, and data, and the fraud schemes that undermine financial integrity and consumer trust.

In this chapter, we'll take a closer look at specific types of bot-driven attacks that online businesses face every day. Each type of bot attack presents unique challenges, affecting operations in ways that range from service disruptions and data theft to direct financial losses.

Cybersecurity Threats

These bot attacks target the security of digital infrastructure by exploiting vulnerabilities, overwhelming resources, or breaching data protection measures. The primary focus of cybersecurity threats is to compromise a business's digital integrity, often resulting in disruptions, data loss, or unauthorized access.

Vulnerability Scanning

Vulnerability scanning is the automated process of identifying security weaknesses in network devices or applications. While most companies run vulnerability scans on their own assets for security purposes, cybercriminals can also run vulnerability scans on your websites, mobile apps and APIs looking for weaknesses they can exploit.

Layer 7 DDoS Attacks

DDoS stands for distributed denial of service. In Layer 7 DDoS attacks, bad bots will target specific application-layer processes and overwhelm those functions or features until your websites, apps, or APIs either slow down significantly or crash altogether. In 2017, Neustar estimated that these attacks cost an organization an average of $2.5 million in revenue.[1]

Layer 7 DDoS Attack Flow

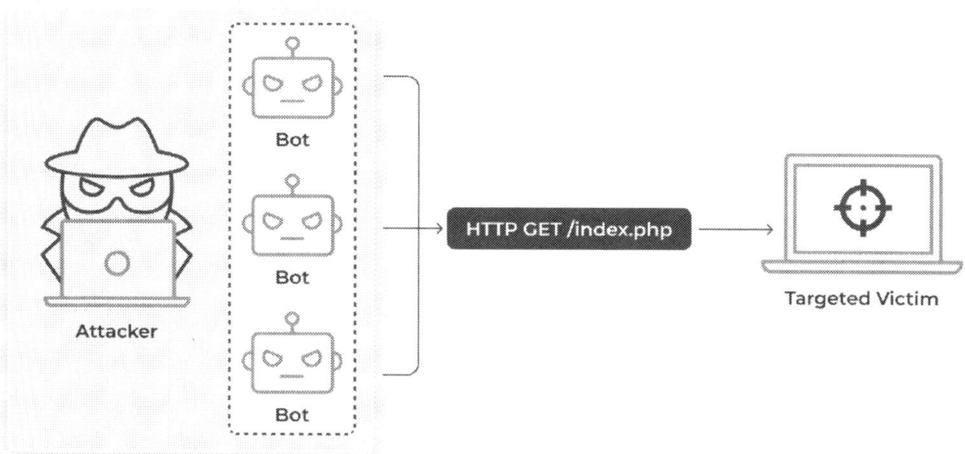

Web Scraping

Scraper bots will steal prices, product descriptions, or other valuable content from your website and use it elsewhere without your permission. Competitors can use scraper bots to collect, analyze and undercut your prices, stealing customers that should have been yours.

Web scraping is also widely used for content theft. When competitors or other unscrupulous actors steal and repurpose your content, it can give them an unfair advantage and hurt your search engine rankings.

The rise of Large Language Model (LLM)-based tools like ChatGPT marks a new era of complexity in content theft. These tools are powered by scraping

1 https://www.businesswire.com/news/home/20170502005553/en/Neustar-Research-Shows-a-DDoS-Attack-Can-Cost-an-Organization-on-Average-More-Than-2.5-Million-in-Revenue

Web Scraping Flow

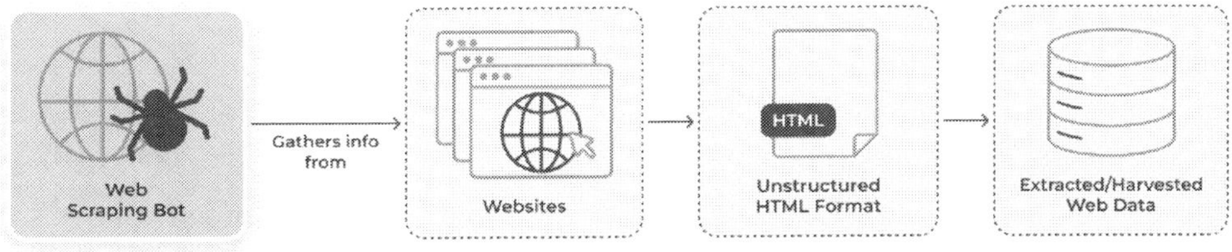

the web, and your own website is no exception. This not only challenges copyright protections but also poses serious risks to data privacy, competitive positioning, and intellectual property rights. These tools further complicate the landscape by potentially monetizing your content through their platforms.

Traditional security measures struggle to accurately detect and counter LLM-driven content scraping, and to distinguish between benign and malicious scraping activities. Malicious LLMs, capable of rapidly collecting vast data, not only devalue proprietary content but also empower competitors or bad actors with quick access to data and market trends. We will discuss LLM scraping in more detail in Chapter 4.

Spam

Bad bots can swarm your website to post bad comments, advertise illicit goods and services or distribute malware. They can also scrape your website for email addresses that they'll then send unsolicited emails to. While often more a nuisance than a genuine threat, spam can still damage your reputation and drain your resources.

Fraud Risks

Cyberfraud is the term for all illegal online activities that deceive people or organizations. Bot-driven fraud threats primarily focus on financial gain through unauthorized transactions, account breaches, or manipulation of digital services. Bot-driven fraud schemes can result in significant financial loss, regulatory issues, and a tarnished brand image.

Payment Fraud

Payment fraud happens when a cybercriminal steals or obtains stolen payment information and uses that information to make unauthorized transactions. The criminal manages to figure out just enough details to purchase goods and services using the victim's data. If you don't detect the fraud, you will process the payment and send the goods or services to the criminal. The victim will eventually discover the unauthorized transaction and ask for a chargeback, and you will incur the chargeback cost, payment processor fees, and the cost of the lost goods or services.

Bot-driven payment fraud includes carding and card cracking. Cybercriminals leverage the firepower of credit card bots to test stolen card data against your payment interface to identify valid card details or missing values of stolen payment card information in order to commit carding fraud.

In carding attacks, cybercriminals use bots to test the validity of stolen card data, often with small transactions to avoid drawing attention.

Card cracking, also known as "card testing", is a type of brute force attack against the payment interface of e-commerce websites. Fraudsters use this method to guess missing values for stolen credit or debit card data, such as the expiration date, the card security code (CSC), and the card identification number (CID).

Carding Attack Flow

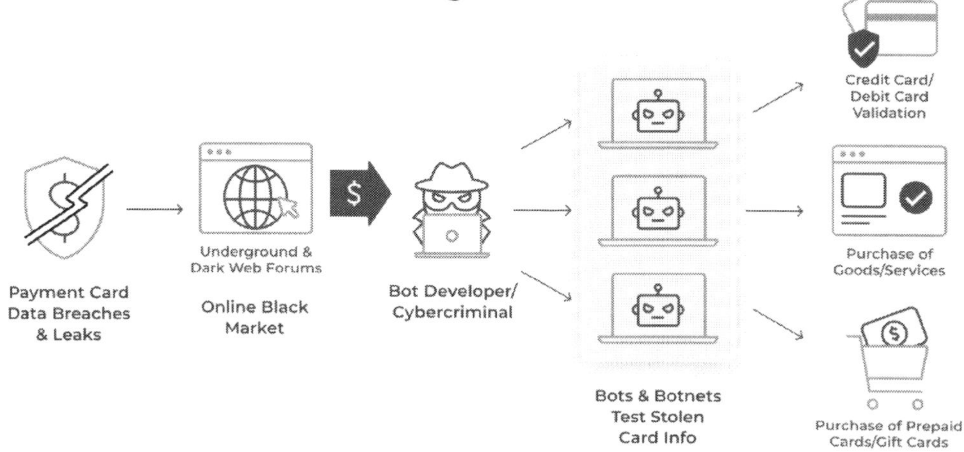

Once they have identified valid cards, fraudsters either sell the compromised payment account details through carding sites on the dark web, or cash out themselves.

Scalping

A scalper bot is an automated program that purchases limited-edition goods (such as popular sneakers or event tickets) to resell them with a profit. Because bots can complete the checkout process in a fraction of the time it takes a human user, they can buy thousands of items the moment they go on sale. Scalping frustrates legitimate customers, consumes bandwidth, drives up infrastructure costs, and keeps IT teams busy firefighting instead of creating value.

Credential Stuffing

Credential stuffing is an automated threat that uses malicious bots to "stuff" known usernames and passwords (typically sourced from data breaches) into online login pages. Because hundreds of millions of accounts worldwide are exposed every year, and because people tend to reuse passwords across websites, hackers often succeed in gaining access to user accounts with a credential stuffing attack.

Account Fraud

Accounts stand at the heart of the e-commerce universe, holding a wealth of user activity, payment details, recommendations, purchase history, and other crucial information that fuels customer relationships.

Account fraud, the deceptive or illegal practice of obtaining unauthorized access to financial or personal accounts, consists primarily of:

1. account takeover
2. fake account creation
3. new account fraud

Given the pivotal role of accounts, any compromise due to account fraud yields detrimental outcomes. ATO and fake account creation can have a slew of negative consequences for enterprises and their customers, including damage to your brand reputation, financial loss, regulatory fines, and more.

Account Takeover (ATO)

On July 15 2020, Barack Obama decided to promote Bitcoin. He tweeted that if you would send him any amount of Bitcoin, he would send back double the amount. He wasn't the only one this generous. On the same day, Kanye West, Bill Gates, Warren Buffett, Joe Biden, Uber, Apple, Wendy's, and over a hundred other high-profile Twitter accounts sent out similar tweets.

The dark web: what is it, and how does it work?

The dark web refers to the section of the internet intentionally and securely hidden from view on "darknets", or overlay networks that require specific browsers, authorizations, or configurations for access. The dark web is not indexed by traditional search engines, and its users are virtually untraceable.

The dark web is often associated with illegal activities such as human trafficking or the buying and selling of drugs, weapons, forged documents, government secrets, and other illicit goods. However, it is also used by privacy-conscious individuals and organizations seeking to avoid surveillance and censorship.

Many cybercriminals rely heavily on the dark web to conduct their unlawful activity. The dark web is a common source for malware (malicious software), and for tools and resources used for fraudulent purposes.

For example, on the dark web, fraudsters can purchase vast databases of stolen account credentials, credit card numbers, or other sensitive data. The compromised data are then used for credential stuffing, account takeover, carding, and other types of bot attacks. Other resources include Bots-as-a-Service offers, proxy pools, and toolkits for bypassing two-factor authentication.

Cybersecurity researchers continuously monitor the dark web for stolen data and emerging trends. By infiltrating dark web forums and marketplaces, they can gather useful intelligence on criminal networks and new attack methods.

Of course, it was a scam. These tweets were sent out as part of a powerful account takeover attack on Twitter. The company was left scrambling. As a temporary solution, they blocked all their verified accounts—their most powerful influencers—from tweeting. It was a huge breach of trust that was in the news for days on end.

Social media companies such as Twitter (now X) aren't the only ones that suffer from account takeovers. Any company with an app or website where users can create accounts is subject to this type of attack, especially if they store credit or debit card details. An ATO attack isn't usually as visible as the one on Twitter either. They tend to fly under the radar until it's too late, after which they can hurt you substantially more than it did Twitter.

Account takeover (ATO) occurs when criminals gain access to a person's online account (through attacks like credential stuffing). Usually, the attacker will change the login credentials to lock the original owner out of their own account. Methods vary, but all account takeover attacks use bots to automate the process:

- They buy (or download for free) databases of stolen login credentials on the dark web.
- They program bots to attack the login endpoints of websites with valuable user accounts.
- The bots very rapidly test all the stolen login-password combinations ("credential stuffing").
- They get access to accounts created with reused credentials.
- They collect personal data and/or exploit means of payment, loyalty points, gift cards etc. associated with the hacked accounts.

Corporate account takeover (CATO) is a specific type of fraud where cybercriminals gain unauthorized access to any kind of account associated with a business instead of an individual, whether that's a corporate email account, user account, social media account, or bank account.

Cybercriminals gain access using a wide variety of techniques, from phishing to malware to social engineering. No industry is safe from this, although it's particularly prominent in the finance, retail, and healthcare industries.

Credential Stuffing and Account Takeover Attack Flow

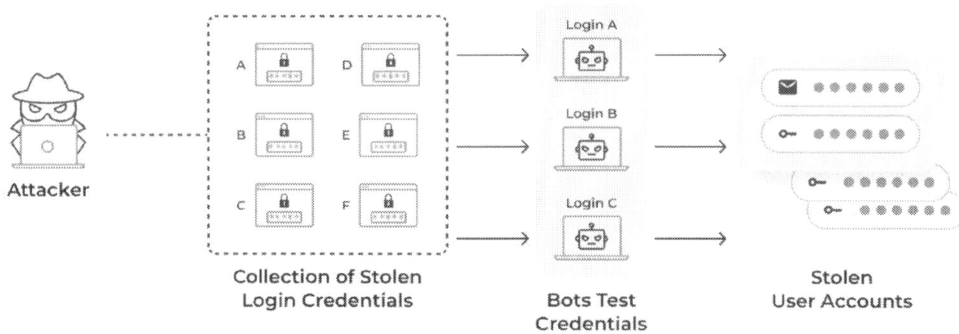

Fake Account Creation

Fake account creation uses bots to automate the creation of fraudulent user accounts. The fake accounts are then used to commit account fraud by generating spam, spreading misinformation or malware, abusing signup bonuses, influencing reviews, voting, and more.

Fake account creation started manually as a way for individuals to remain anonymous and avoid spam. But after some time, it became a way to abuse bonus offers or pretend to be someone else, such as in romance scams (aka "catfishing").

Today, fake accounts are often associated with social media (such as bots trying to influence elections on X, formerly Twitter), but there are many other use cases. The use of fake accounts to influence product reviews, for example, is now so widespread that it has become a flourishing industry of its own.

In the gaming and gambling industry, fake accounts are often used to profit from signup bonuses, coupons, or other benefits that can subsequently be monetized.

Other examples include the manipulation of survey results, money laundering, or misusing free services (e.g. exploiting a free cloud computing account offer to mine cryptocurrency).

Fake Account Registrations by Bots

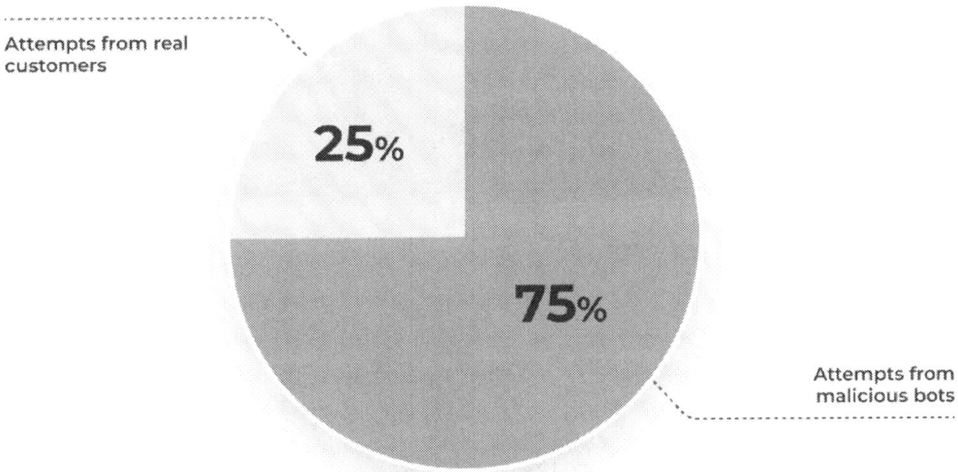

For a leading luxury brand, DataDome detected that 75% of registration attempts to book an appointment on their website were made by malicious bots.

Finally, attackers can use fake accounts to camouflage credential stuffing attacks, by logging in with large numbers of "legitimate" accounts (with known usernames and passwords) that will lower the login fail rate of the attack.

New Account Fraud

New account fraud is the use of stolen (or synthetic) identities to create new accounts. It is an increasingly common type of fraud that can have far-reaching consequences for your business, from financial loss to reputational damage.

Fraudsters use a variety of sophisticated techniques to create new accounts, often through both technological vulnerabilities and human errors. These techniques range from stealing real identities to fabricating entirely new ones, each with its unique approach and challenges in detection and prevention.

Identity Theft: This involves fraudsters obtaining personal information of real individuals, such as social security numbers, addresses, and birthdates, often through data breaches, mail theft, or dumpster diving. They use this information to open new accounts, masquerading as the individual whose identity they have stolen. It leads to unauthorized financial transactions and credit applications.

Synthetic Identity Fraud: With this method, fraudsters combine real and fake information to create a new, fictitious identity. For example, they might use a real social security number with a fabricated name and address. These synthetic identities are harder to detect because they aren't real people but they seem like they are. Synthetic identities are often used to establish credit histories and commit fraud over time.

Credit Card Fraud: This type of fraud involves using stolen credit card information to open new accounts or access existing ones. Fraudsters might obtain this information through skimming devices, hacking into databases, or phishing scams, and then use it to make unauthorized purchases or cash withdrawals.

According to a 2023 report from Javelin Strategy & Research, businesses lost an estimated **$20 billion** to new account fraud in 2022.[2] These losses stem not just from the fraudulent transactions themselves but also from the resources spent in detecting, addressing, and preventing this type of fraud. This includes investments in security measures like account takeover protection and the operational costs associated with resolving fraud cases.

Phishing: Phishing is a technique where fraudsters trick individuals into revealing personal information through fake emails, websites, or phone calls that appear to be from legitimate sources. This information is then used to create new accounts or access existing accounts fraudulently. Phishing often targets not only personal details, but also login credentials for online services.

New account fraud can devastate your business financially, damage your reputation, complicate regulatory compliance, and erode customer trust.

2 https://javelinstrategy.com/research/2023-identity-fraud-study-butterfly-effect

Click Fraud Attack Flow

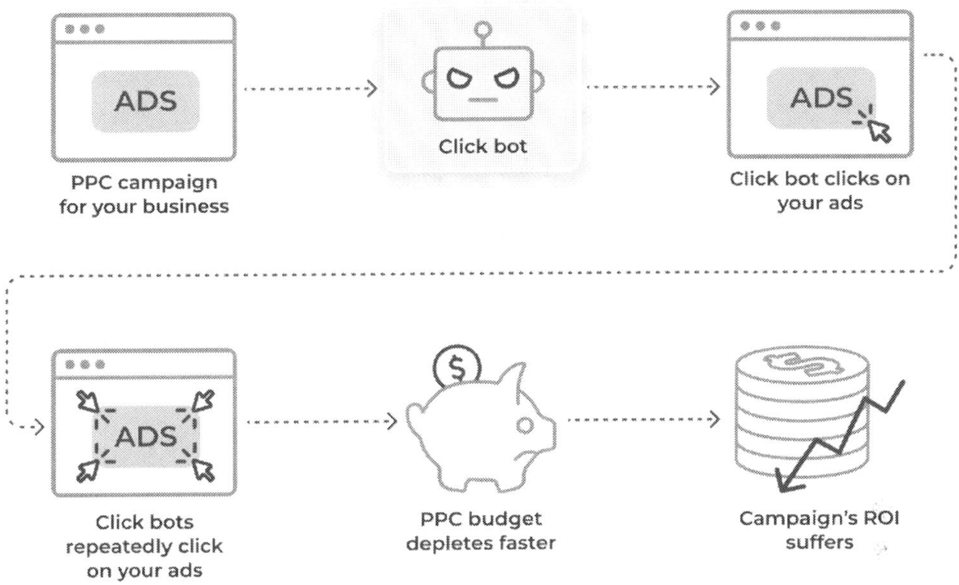

Ad Fraud

Ad or click fraud means generating fake pageviews, clicks, and impressions to cost advertisers money without generating any sales. Bad bots do this at such a scale, it costs companies billions of dollars a year. This is bad for advertisers as well as publishers, which want to maintain good relationships with their advertisers. Click fraud can seriously damage their reputation.

Ad fraud involves falsifying the number of times an online advertisement is clicked on or displayed. Scammers trick advertising platforms with fraudulent traffic, clicks, impressions, conversions, and other data events, preventing websites from delivering content to real users. The fraudsters reap financial gain because the advertisers pay even though the ads never reach the intended audience. Further, it can negatively impact brand reputation.

Since ad fraud generates activity that doesn't come from a real user, it's also called invalid traffic (IVT). There are two main types of IVT:

- **General invalid traffic (GIVT):** identifiable through regular filtration activities, like lists or other standard checks.
- **Sophisticated invalid traffic (SIVT):** only identifiable using advanced analytics, multi-point collaboration, and/or human intervention.

How Bots Skew Your Marketing Analytics

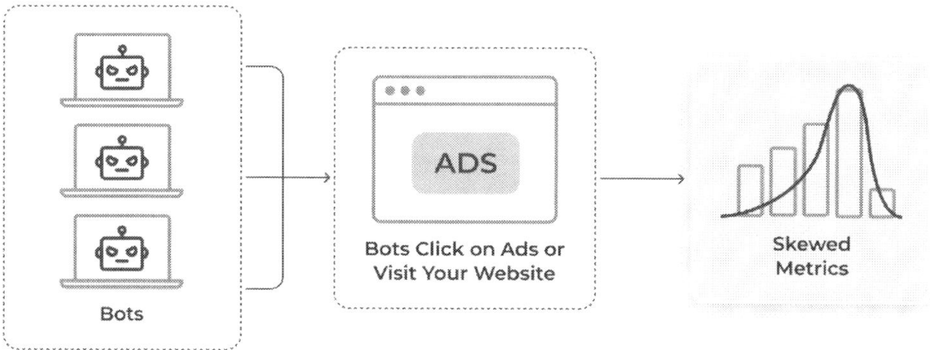

Fraudsters can use a multitude of different tactics:

Cookie Stuffing: Cookies are small bits of code that track user behavior, providing insight into your ad campaigns' success. They can tell you whether the effort led to a conversion where someone made a purchase or give you feedback about users' interests. Fraudsters can use cookie stuffing in two different ways:

- Inserting a cookie from a different website than the one the user originally visited to change the attribution and payment model
- Placing cookies on a bot so that it looks like the keyword is getting more impressions, ultimately costing more and making the scammers more money

Click Fraud/Bot Fraud: Usually executed by bots, click fraud targets pay-per-click (PPC) ads tricking the ad platform into believing that human users are interacting with the content, making a post or website more popular. Companies then spend more money to place ads on the website, but they're really paying the fraudsters.

For publishers who make money from ads, this might not appear to matter since they're getting paid anyway. However, if advertisers find out, they may decide to pull their ads.

Click Spamming/Click Flooding: This variant specifically targets mobile apps and websites. While the website or app works normally for the user, it executes clicks in the background. Users never even know that they've interacted with in-app ads because they never saw it.

Click Injection: Click injections are a more sophisticated type of click spamming. These target Android apps, enabling scammers to detect when a user downloads apps to earn credit for the installs. While the app installs are real, the fake ad engagement means that advertisers will continue to spend money on the fraudulent advertising partner.

Domain Spoofing: With domain spoofing, fraudsters impersonate a high-value domain that's more valuable and worth more money. While the impressions and users are real, the low-quality website isn't worth the money spent. Some types of domain spoofing include:

- Cross-Domain Embedding
- Custom Browsers
- Human Browsers

Pixel Stuffing: When scammers use pixel stuffing, they serve multiple ads in a single pixel frame, making the advertisements invisible to users. Even if the ads are delivered, the users don't actually see them, so the advertiser gets no value from them.

Ad Injection: This type of impression online ad fraud inserts new ads or replaces current ones while someone is on the internet. Sometimes one ad is inserted on top of existing ones. Sometimes they replace them entirely or make them show up on pages that weren't supposed to have ads. Often, this type of ad fraud occurs after malware is delivered to the user when they install a browser, extension, or app.

Ad Stacking: With this mobile ad fraud variant, scammers "hide" advertisements. Multiple ads are layered on top of each other, with only one visible to users. This is another case where the impressions may be real for all ads in the stack, but users won't see the content, meaning the advertiser doesn't get value.

Geo Masking/Location Fraud: Part of using ad networks is getting the right content to the right people. For many marketers, this means hitting a target geographic location. With geo masking, fraudsters send false location data so that the ad serves outside the targeted demographic.

User-Agent Spoofing: Scammers manipulate the header that is in the web page request to obfuscate information about the user's browser. Fraudsters often use this tactic to hide bots.

SDK Spoofing: Connected to network interception attacks, SDK spoofing happens when a fraudster breaks the SSL encryption to learn what URL calls represent in-app action so that they can generate fake installs.

Install Farms: Using either bots or emulator programs, scammers use real devices that click on advertisements or install applications. This makes it look like real users are installing the software, when in reality no one is seeing the advertisements.

Forced Redirect Ads: Beyond stealing revenue, malicious actors can use online ad fraud to deliver malware by embedding a malicious ad or iframe on a webpage. This redirects users to a site that contains malware or spyware, attempting to steal personally identifiable information.

Ad fraud is hard to detect because it may not have an immediate, obvious financial impact. You might just think that your ad campaign is successful, continuing to spend more money on it. In reality, you're getting fake leads and not reaching potential customers. Meanwhile, the criminals continue to reap the benefits.

CHAPTER 3: A BRIEF HISTORY OF BOT TECHNOLOGY

The evolution of bot technology reflects the ongoing arms race between attackers and defenders. In the early days, bots were basic, primarily used for automating repetitive tasks like web scraping or simple data extraction. These bots were easy to detect and block using primitive defenses such as IP deny lists or simple rate-limiting techniques.

However, as web technologies advanced, so did bot capabilities. Bots began mimicking human behaviors—performing tasks such as filling out forms, clicking buttons, and navigating complex user interfaces. Alongside this, attackers sought ways to conceal their bots' origins, allowing them to blend in with legitimate user traffic and avoid detection.

Early Bots: Basic Automation

In the early days, bots were simple scripts created to automate repetitive tasks. They were often written in languages like Perl or Python and used basic HTTP requests to interact with web pages. These bots could fetch web pages using tools like curl or wget, scrape content, and automate simple interactions.

Early malicious bots were primarily used for spamming and basic scraping. They sent HTTP requests to web servers to fetch pages and then parsed the HTML to extract email addresses or other desired information. These bots operated without much sophistication, making them relatively easy to detect and block using basic IP deny listing, rate limiting techniques or lack of JavaScript rendering.

The Rise of Headless Browsers

As web technologies advanced, so did the complexity of bots. Traditional scraping methods became less effective with the advent of JavaScript-heavy websites and dynamic content loading via AJAX. This led to the adoption of headless browsers—browsers that run without a graphical user interface.

Headless browsers marked a significant leap in bot capabilities. Tools like PhantomJS and Selenium allowed bots to execute JavaScript, interact with dynamic content, and render web pages as a human user would. They could perform actions such as filling out forms, clicking buttons, and navigating through multi-step processes.

This made them ideal for automating tasks like account creation and login attempts, which were previously difficult to achieve with simple HTTP requests. However, there were plenty of open-source tests to detect them, and detection was quite easy.

Then, in 2017, Chrome released its official headless mode, allowing Chrome to be launched and automated without displaying a visible browser window. It dramatically improved performance and scalability for bot developers.

Mimicking Human Behavior

To evade detection, bots began incorporating techniques to mimic human behavior more closely. This included things like simulating mouse movements and keystrokes, or randomized delays between actions.

Advanced bots started to use libraries like Puppeteer to control headless Chrome browsers, making their behavior nearly indistinguishable from that of a real user. Automation libraries have consistent HTTP headers (because they are browsers), consistent TLS fingerprints, and so on, which means that it requires expert knowledge to detect them.

Open-source libraries like Puppeteer Extra Stealth, which forge fingerprints very realistically, also made it a lot easier to create realistic bots and a lot more difficult to detect them.

Access to Millions of (Residential) IPs

In parallel with their advancements in browser technology, bot developers also started using residential proxies to mask their IP addresses and avoid being blocked. By routing their traffic through a network of legitimate IP addresses, these bots can blend in with normal user traffic. Many also use IP rotation techniques, switching IP addresses frequently to avoid detection.

Thanks to residential proxy services such as Brightdata, Smartproxy, and Oxylabs, bot developers now have access to millions of residential IPs located all around the world.

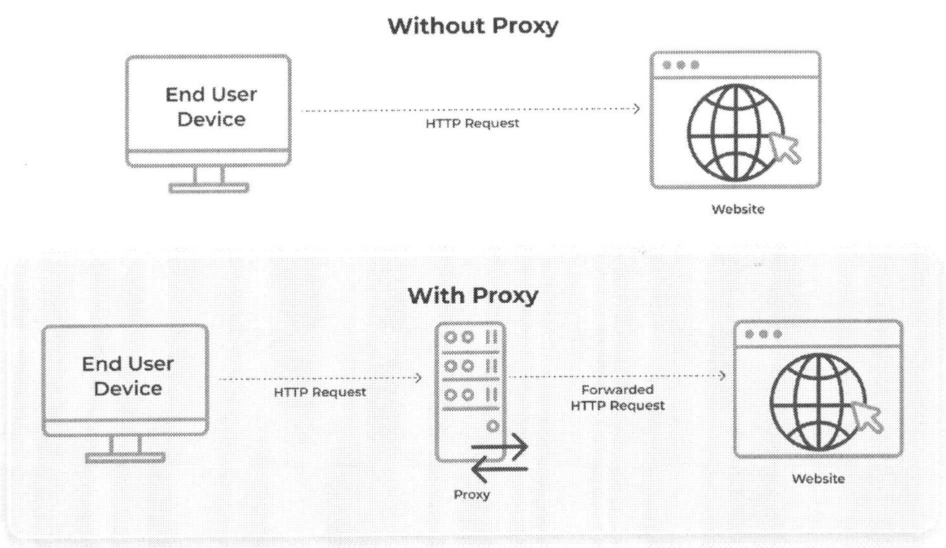

This enables bot developers to:

- **Distribute their attacks** across thousands of IPs, which help them to bypass IP-based rate limiting techniques.
- Use **IPs that belong to well-known ISPs** such as Comcast and AT&T, which help them to bypass all forms of detection that aim to block data center IPs.
- Use **IPs located in the same country as the target** website or mobile app. In this way, they can bypass all kinds of geo-blocking techniques.

Bots as a Service (BaaS)

In the past, developing and executing cyberattacks required technical skill. Now, that's no longer necessarily the case. Thanks to a rise in "bots as a service" (BaaS), fraudsters can simply outsource bot creation. Bots as a service allows anyone to one-stop-shop for malicious bots in exchange for a subscription fee, with different levels of pricing and service offered. Some BaaS providers will set up a botnet for you, offer how-to guides, provide 24/7 support and provide a guaranteed hit rate.

BaaS developers usually structure their pricing model so that their users only pay for successful requests (those that return a 200 HTTP response code). This means that they incentivize themselves to build ever more capable, dangerous bots—and the skyrocketing ROI justifies bot haute couture.

Site-Specific Bots

Most bots are general-use tools that can be used on multiple platforms and sites. But as bot protection has become more effective, developers have found a new way to avoid easy detection: site-specific bots, hand-crafted for use on one website, mobile app, or API.

Site-specific bots can be better programmed to ensure their behavior and fingerprints match more closely with the human customers that normally use the site, app, or API.

Some bots are attack-specific (rather than site-specific), crafted for a certain attack type, such as scalping or scraping. These bots are fully invested in making their attacks pay off, either for the bot developer, the customer using the bot as a service (BaaS), or both.

<•••>

As bot developers refine their capabilities in human-like behavior and human-like IP addresses, a new battlefront is emerging: artificial intelligence (AI). While browser technology and IP address manipulation remain crucial in making bots resemble legitimate users, AI is transforming how both attackers and defenders operate.

In the next chapter, we will explore how AI is being harnessed to elevate the sophistication of bots, introducing additional challenges for defenders.

CHAPTER 4: AI, THE NEXT EMERGING BATTLEFRONT

Today, the most advanced bots incorporate artificial intelligence (AI) and machine learning to enhance their capabilities. These bots can analyze and learn from patterns in web traffic, adapting their behavior to avoid detection. For instance, machine learning algorithms can help bots better mimic human browsing habits or find new ways to bypass CAPTCHA systems.

AI tools also greatly facilitate tasks like fake content creation, fake comments or customer reviews, fake logins, etc. In terms of online security, AI can not only make new types of attacks possible but also make existing ones more efficient and harder to detect.

In this chapter, we will discuss the ways in which AI enhances a bot's ability to mimic human behavior and for fraudsters to scale their attacks.

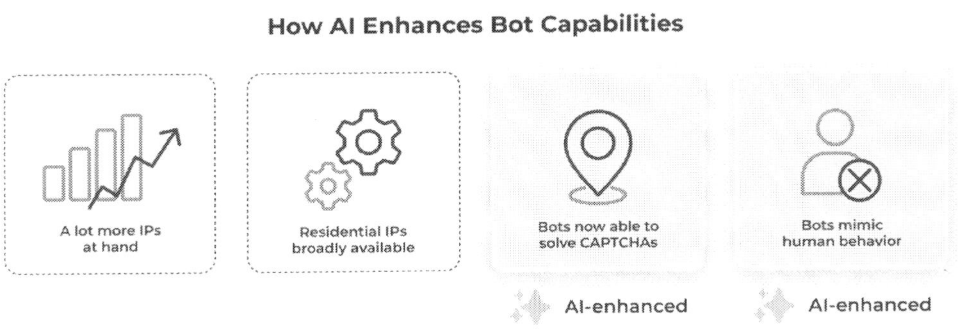

The AI "Gold Rush" in Cybersecurity

In recent years, the hype around AI in cybersecurity has reached a fever pitch, similar to the surge of interest around Zero Trust frameworks a few years ago. This excitement is not unfounded; AI promises to revolutionize many aspects of security, both in terms of defense and attack strategies.

A significant fear factor revolves around the potential for attackers to use AI asynchronously, leveraging unknown capabilities to outsmart defenders. This fear is compounded by the rapid sophistication of bot attacks, even before the widespread adoption of AI.

AI-Enhanced Bot Capabilities

Machine learning (ML) and artificial intelligence (AI) technologies are being harnessed by fraudsters to create more sophisticated and effective bot attacks. These technologies enable bots to perform complex tasks and adapt to defenses more efficiently.

- **Automated Data Analysis:** AI and ML can be used to parse large amounts of data, such as HTML content, and automatically generate CSS selectors. This enables bots to accurately target specific elements on a webpage, enhancing their scraping and interaction capabilities.
- **Image and Audio Recognition:** Advanced bots can use AI-driven image and audio recognition techniques to bypass security measures like CAPTCHAs. By interpreting visual and audio challenges that are designed to differentiate humans from bots, these bots can successfully navigate through security barriers.
- **Tailored Spam Generation:** Large Language Models (LLMs) can be employed to generate spam content that is customized for the targeted website. By analyzing the specific context and language used on the site, these bots can create more convincing and effective spam messages, increasing the likelihood of successful phishing or fraud attempts.
- **Generating realistic human behavior:** Attackers can use generative adversarial network approaches to generate human-looking behavior, particularly mouse movements.

- **Real-Time Adaptation:** Bots can use AI to analyze the responses they get from security systems, adjusting their methods on-the-fly to avoid detection. This ability to rapidly adapt makes them a formidable threat, as they can continuously refine their tactics based on the defenses they encounter.

Data Scraping & Large Language Model Training

Even when they are not used for deliberately malicious attacks, the fact that ChatGPT and other large language models (LLMs) are trained on vast amounts of data scraped from the internet without permission has created new ethical concerns and complications in the online threat landscape.

3 Risks Presented by LLMs, ChatGPT, & ChatGPT Plugins

Among the threats ChatGPT and ChatGPT plugins can pose against online businesses, there are three key risks:

Content theft (or republishing data without permission from the original source) can hurt the authority, SEO rankings, and perceived value of your original content.

Reduced traffic to your website or app becomes problematic, as users getting answers directly through ChatGPT and its plugins no longer need to find or visit your pages.

Data breaches, or even the accidental broad distribution of sensitive data, are becoming more likely by the second. Not all "public-facing" data is intended to be redistributed or shared outside of the original context, but scrapers do not know the difference. The results can include anything from a loss in competitive advantage to severe damages to your brand reputation.

Depending on your business model, your company should consider ways to opt out of having your data used to train LLMs.

How ChatGPT Gets Training Data

According to a research paper published by OpenAI, ChatGPT3 was trained on several datasets:

- Common Crawl
- WebText2
- Books1 and Books2
- Wikipedia

The largest amount of training data comes from Common Crawl, which provides access to web information through an open repository of web crawl data. The Common Crawl crawler bot, also known as CCBot, leverages Apache Nutch to enable developers to build large-scale scrapers.

The most current version of CCBot crawls from Amazon AWS and identifies itself with a user agent of 'CCBot/2.0'. But businesses who want to allow CCBot should not rely solely on the user agent to identify it, because many bad bots spoof their user agents to disguise themselves as good bots and avoid being blocked.

To allow CCBot on your website, use attributes such as IP ranges or reverse DNS. To block ChatGPT, your website should, at minimum, block traffic from CCBot.

3 Ways to Block CCBot

1. Robots.txt: Since CCBot respects robots.txt files, you can block it with the following lines of code:

```
User-agent: CCBot

Disallow: /
```

2. Blocking CCBot User Agent: You can safely block an unwanted bot through user agent. (Note that, in contrast, allowing bot traffic through a user agent can be unsafe, easily abused by attackers.)

3. Bot Management Software: Whether it's for ChatGPT or a dark web database, the best way to prevent bots from scraping your websites, apps, and APIs is with specialized bot protection that uses machine learning to keep up with evolving threat tactics in real time.

Scrapers Can Always Find Workarounds

LLMs use scraper bots to gather training data. While blocking CCBot might be effective for blocking ChatGPT scrapers today, there is no telling what the future holds for LLM scrapers. Moving forward, if too many websites block OpenAI (for example) from accessing their content, the developers could decide to stop respecting robots.txt and could stop declaring their crawler identity in the user agent.

Another possibility is OpenAI could use its partnership with Microsoft to access Microsoft Bing's scraper data, making the situation more challenging for website owners. Bing's bots identify as Bingbot, but blocking them could cause problems by preventing your site from being indexed on the Bing search engine, resulting in fewer human visitors.

You could face similar issues by blocking Google's LLM Bard (competitor to ChatGPT). Google is vague about the origin and collection of the public data used to train Bard, but it is possible that Bard is, or will be, trained with data collected by Googlebot scrapers. Like with Bingbot, blocking Googlebot would likely be unwise, impacting how your website gets indexed and how the Google search engine drives traffic to your site. The result could mean a serious drop in visitors.

Using Plugins to Access Live Data

One of the main limits of models like ChatGPT is the lack of access to live data. Since it was trained on a dataset that stops in 2021, it is unable to provide the most relevant, up-to-date information. That's where plugins come in.

Plugins are used to connect LLMs like ChatGPT to external tools and allow the LLMs to access external data available online, which can include private data and real-time news. Plugins also let users complete actions online (e.g. booking a flight or ordering groceries) through API calls.

Some businesses are developing their own plugins to provide a new way for users to interact with their content/services via ChatGPT. But, depending on your industry, letting users interact with your website through third-party ChatGPT plugins can mean fewer ads seen by your users, as well as lower traffic to your website.

You may also notice that users are less willing to pay for your premium features once your features can be replicated through third-party ChatGPT plugins. For example, an unofficial web client interacting with your site could offer premium features through their UI.

How to Identify ChatGPT Plugin Requests

OpenAI documentation states that requests with a specific user agent HTTP header (with token: "ChatGPT-User") come from ChatGPT plugins. But the documentation does not state that the disclosed user agent is the only user agent that can be used by plugins when making HTTP requests.

Therefore, as ChatGPT plugins interact with third-party APIs, the APIs can then do any kind of HTTP requests from their own infrastructure. The diagram below shows what happens when a fictitious "Live Sport Plugin" is used with ChatGPT to get an update about a sporting event.

How to Identify ChatGPT Plugin Requests

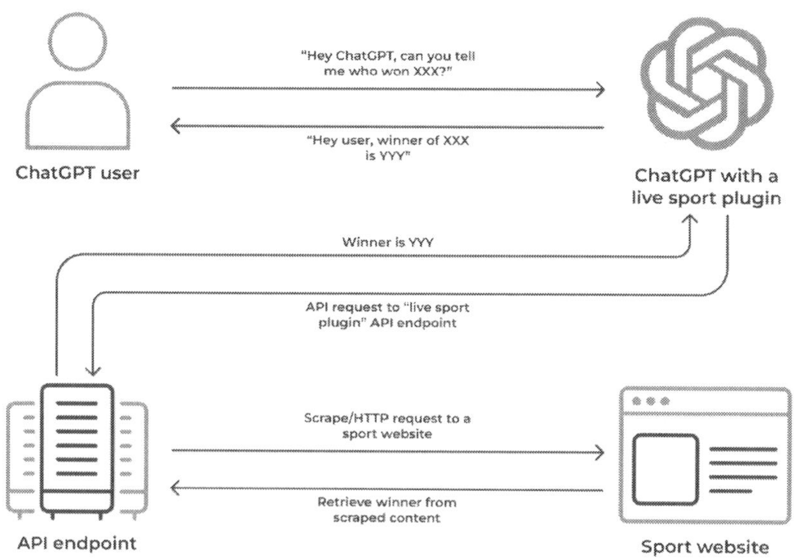

ChatGPT plugin

- ChatGPT triggers the Live Sport Plugin, making a request to the API endpoints based on parameters from the user prompt.
- The plugin makes an HTTP request to scrape a sports website to get the latest information about the event.
- The information is then passed back to the end user through ChatGPT.

A plugin can actually make a request to a sport API without having to scrape the sports website. In fact, when requests are made directly from the server hosting the plugin API, there is no constraint on the user agent.

How to Block ChatGPT Plugin Requests

In a process similar to blocking ChatGPT's web scrapers, you can block requests from plugins that declare their presence with the "ChatGPT-User" substring by user agent. But blocking the user agent could also block ChatGPT users with the "browsing" mode activated. And, contrary to what OpenAI documentation might indicate, blocking requests from "ChatGPT-User" does not guarantee that ChatGPT and its plugins can't reach your data under different user agent tokens.

In fact, ChatGPT plugins can make requests directly from the servers hosting their APIs using any user agent, and even using automated (headless) browsers. Detecting plugins that do not declare their identity in the user agent requires advanced bot detection techniques.

Determining Your Next Steps

Obtaining high-quality datasets of human-generated content will remain of critical importance to LLMs. In the long term, companies like OpenAI (funded partially by Microsoft) and Google may be tempted to use Bingbots and Googlebots to build datasets to train their LLMs. That would make it more difficult for websites to simply opt out of having their data collected, since most online businesses rely heavily on Bing and Google to index their content and drive traffic to their site.

Websites with valuable data will either want to look for ways to monetize the use of their data or opt out of AI model training to avoid losing web traffic and ad revenue to ChatGPT and its plugins. If you wish to opt out, you'll need advanced bot detection techniques, such as fingerprinting, proxy detection, and behavioral analysis, to stop bots before they can access your data.

Advanced solutions for bot and fraud protection leverage AI and machine learning (ML) to detect and stop unfamiliar bots from the first request, keeping your content safe from LLM scrapers, unknown plugins, and other rapidly evolving AI technologies.

The rapid advancement of artificial intelligence, particularly in large language models like ChatGPT, has escalated the complexity of the digital threat landscape. These tools, while groundbreaking, have introduced ethical dilemmas and significant risks to businesses, from unauthorized data scraping to reduced web traffic and competitive disadvantages. The methods outlined in this chapter provide essential strategies for detecting and blocking unwanted AI-driven bots and plugins. However, as AI technology continues to evolve, so must our defenses.

In the next chapter, we'll examine the varied impact of these sophisticated threats across industries, exploring the ripple effects of bot-driven fraud and data misuse on business operations and consumer trust.

CHAPTER 5: BOTS & ONLINE FRAUD ON DIFFERENT INDUSTRIES

The nature of bot activity and online fraud varies significantly across different fields, influencing the way businesses must approach their security measures.

From the relentless bot-driven attacks on e-commerce platforms that seek to manipulate prices and hoard inventory, to the sophisticated fraud schemes plaguing the financial sector, each industry contends with its own set of vulnerabilities. The ticketing industry faces bot-driven attacks aiming to snatch up tickets for popular events, leading to inflated resale prices and frustrated customers, while in the travel sector, automated bots are often used to scrape pricing data and perform fake bookings, disrupting operations and skewing market analytics.

In this chapter, we'll explore how these and other industries are impacted by bot activity and fraudulent behavior.

Ticketing

A ticket scalper is a type of bot specifically programmed to scalp tickets—that is, to purchase as many as possible to later resell at a high markup—to popular events such as musical concerts and sports games. Because bots can perform actions much faster than humans, they're able to buy up huge numbers of tickets before humans can, keeping human users from purchasing tickets at reasonable prices themselves.

One hacker scooped up 30,000 tickets to the Broadway hit "Hamilton" in 2015-2016 and another 1,000+ tickets to a U2 concert—in less than 60 seconds each time. In another attack, a malicious bot acquired 520 Beyoncé concert tickets within three minutes.

More recently, Taylor Swift fans (aka "Swifties") worldwide were left heartbroken when they were unable to beat the scalper bots plaguing Ticketmaster's site, a frustrating situation for all.

Cybercriminals can make some serious cash using ticket bots. Online event ticket sales reached $71B in 2023, and the global online event ticketing market size is expected to hit $68B by 2025—and scalped tickets are often sold at markups of up to 50 percent. The high-level ROI tempts more nefarious hackers every day to try gaming the system.

Other attackers, which are simply looking to cause mayhem or harm the reputation of a competitor, may not even sell the tickets. For some bots, the goal is to cause a denial of inventory while malicious actors sit back and watch the chaos unfold.

The Taylor Swift ticket attack is a prime example of both the increasing sophistication of bots—which even managed to disrupt Ticketmaster's "Verified Fan" presale—and the massive payday threat actors see in scalping tickets.

The primary lesson here is to ensure your business and customers are secured by adaptive and thorough bot protection that covers all endpoints across your mobile apps, websites, and APIs. As high profile events and special edition goods inevitably continue to launch, expect bots to make their best attempt at disrupting your sales, creating chaos.

Airlines

In 2020, payment fraud cost airlines ~1.2% of annual revenue, or around $1 billion every year.[1] That number has only increased as more people travel around the world—and as more people look for too-good-to-be-true deals on travel and hotels. Airline fraud attacks have a 60% correlation with the average

1 https://www.iata.org/contentassets/8a1d401955164c868258e7875edd5d5a/iata_whitepaper_fraud_july2020_digital_en.pdf

transaction amount,[2] showing that higher transaction costs are more likely to be targeted by fraudsters.

Often, fraudsters are targeting airline tickets themselves through online travel booking platforms, looking for cheap ways to fund a vacation. Cybercriminals abuse loyalty programs, stolen credit card numbers, and other personal data to book a trip for free.

CASE STUDY

PROTECTING FAIR ACCESS FOR PATRONS

The Pittsburgh Cultural Trust was struggling with rampant automated bot attacks aimed at buying event tickets for resale at inflated prices, a practice known as scalping. This influx of automated traffic not only deprived genuine patrons of fair access to tickets but also caused financial losses through chargebacks and increased infrastructure costs.

Initially, their mitigation efforts fell short. The existing solution lacked effective anti-scalping measures, relying heavily on manual identification of suspicious activities. This manual approach was time-consuming and often ineffective, allowing scalpers to exploit vulnerabilities repeatedly.

The consequences were profound. Tickets frequently ended up on secondary markets, creating barriers for genuine customers and undermining the Trust's revenue streams. The continuous barrage of bot traffic strained their website infrastructure, necessitating additional server capacity to manage the load.

In response to these challenges, the Trust sought a more robust solution capable of identifying and thwarting scalping bots in real-time. This led them to implement a new system that not only targeted scalping but also addressed other forms of fraudulent activity like credential stuffing and DDoS attacks. The successful implementation significantly curtailed bot-driven scalping attempts, ensuring a fairer ticket purchasing process for genuine patrons and alleviating the financial strain caused by fraudulent transactions and excess infrastructure costs.

2 https://fraud.net/wp-content/uploads/sites/2/2020/02/Fraud.net-2020-Travel-Industry-Report-Final-200217.pdf

Airlines that do nothing to prevent travel fraud are likely to see direct losses from fraudulent bookings, chargebacks, and unauthorized transactions, as well as operational costs from investigating fraud cases.

Fraud also damages customer trust, as travelers will be hesitant to book through the business again, and brand image will be impacted by negative publicity.

Fraud can disrupt normal operations and lead to service delays or cancellations. Additionally, customer support teams handling fraud cases will likely have longer response times—and lower customer satisfaction.

Other Travel & Hospitality Businesses

The travel and hospitality industry faces significant financial risks from online fraud and cyberattacks, such as booking fraud, account takeovers, and data breaches. Notorious attacks such as the Marriott International data breach and the Carnival Corporation ransomware incident highlight the severity of these threats.

According to the DataDome Bot Security Report 2024, a staggering 91% of travel websites are not protected against simple bot attacks. Businesses in this sector must understand the cost implications of bot-driven cybersecurity threats and the return on investment (ROI) of implementing an online fraud solution.

Payment fraud, booking fraud, and account takeovers can lead to substantial revenue losses. These fraudulent activities cost businesses money and block legitimate customers from making bookings.

Addressing the aftermath of a cyberattack or remediating fraudulent activity often involves significant expenses, including IT recovery efforts, customer support, and potential legal fees. High bot traffic can also cause rising infrastructure costs and strain your systems. Automated cybersecurity solutions reduce the need for manual intervention, freeing up resources and enabling teams to focus on strategic initiatives.

Failure to comply with data protection regulations like GDPR can result in hefty fines. For example, the cost of non-compliance with GDPR can reach up to €20 million or 4% of the annual global turnover, whichever is higher. Informing customers about data breaches involves considerable costs, including notification logistics and potential compensation. Having the right security and fraud prevention solutions can save you from paying fines down the road.

Finally, a single security breach can significantly damage a travel brand's reputation, leading to a long-term decline in customer trust and loyalty. In addition, the media coverage of cyber incidents can lead to negative publicity, affecting the brand's image and search results.

E-Commerce

The e-commerce sector, which is characterized by its competitive nature and high volume of transactions, is a prime target for bot-driven fraud and cyberattacks.

Carding is a type of attack where the cybercriminals use bots to test the validity of stolen card data, often with small transactions to avoid drawing attention. A card testing attack enables a credit card bot to test large numbers of cards within a short time span. The method is used to test not only payment cards, but also gift cards and vouchers.

Card cracking is when a fraudster has gained access to some, but not all, stolen credit card credentials. Attackers who attempt card testing fraud typically don't know two things:

- Whether the card is still valid (not blocked yet) and can still be used to successfully complete a transaction.
- The limit of the credit card, or the maximum amount of money they can use on the card to purchase goods.

To find out, the fraudster will then test the card by making small purchases on e-commerce sites. Once a transaction has been approved, the fraudster will then move on to making bigger purchases and will try to get as much value as possible from each card.

Account takeover (ATO) occurs when a cybercriminal gains access to a legitimate user account on an e-commerce store and uses the account to make a purchase. ATO fraud can cause serious damage for both the e-commerce store (retailer) and the customers. For customers, ATO may result in more serious identity theft attacks, and the customer might blame the e-commerce store.

Denial of inventory, aka "inventory hoarding", is a type of cybersecurity attack where an automated script, or "shopping bot" repeatedly places an

CASE STUDY

PUTTING AN END TO CARDING FRAUD

Pierre Fabre USA, part of the global pharmaceutical and dermo-cosmetics company, was facing carding fraud on its e-commerce platforms. Carding attacks involve bots using stolen credit card information to make small purchases, testing the validity of the cards. For Pierre Fabre, this led to a surge in fraudulent transactions, which not only resulted in direct financial losses but also created a cascade of additional problems.

These fraudulent activities increased chargebacks, which strained their relationship with payment processors and threatened to raise transaction fees. The attacks also risked damaging the company's reputation, as customers could lose trust if they became aware of security vulnerabilities. Moreover, the operational burden of dealing with these fraudulent transactions was significant, requiring additional resources to detect and reverse unauthorized payments.

To address these threats, Pierre Fabre USA implemented a sophisticated bot management solution designed to identify and block malicious traffic in real time. This solution effectively curbed the carding attacks, reducing the number of fraudulent transactions and protecting the company's financial standing and customer trust.

This case underscores the critical importance of protecting e-commerce platforms from bot-driven fraud, particularly in industries where customer security and trust are paramount. Advanced solutions like those offered by DataDome are essential for maintaining secure transactions and safeguarding a company's reputation and financial health.

e-commerce product or service in the shopping cart without ever completing the transaction. This tricks the e-commerce site to believe that the product or service is out of stock, so that legitimate buyers will see it as not being available.

Financial Services

This sector is a prime target due to the high value of transactions and the sensitive nature of financial data. Banks face the challenge of balancing stringent security measures with a seamless customer experience.

New account fraud is a type of identity theft where fraudsters use stolen or fabricated personal information to open new accounts that seem legitimate but are ultimately used for illegal purposes. Fraudsters often use new account fraud to launder money, finance illicit activities, or commit credit fraud.

Fraudsters use a variety of sophisticated techniques to create new accounts, often through both technological vulnerabilities and human errors. These techniques range from stealing real identities to fabricating entirely new ones, each with its unique approach and challenges in detection and prevention.

Credential harvesting, also known as password harvesting or username harvesting, is a cyberattack technique that involves stealing personal or financial data from users. This data can include usernames, passwords, credit card data, user IDs, and email addresses.

Cybercriminals have various ways of obtaining such sensitive information, like bot fraud, phishing emails, fake websites, social engineering techniques that exploit human vulnerabilities, and many more. Once the cybercriminals have obtained these stolen credentials, they will use them to gain unauthorized access to personal accounts or corporate networks. Credential harvesting then becomes the gateway to many different types of online fraud.

Classified Ads

The online classified ads sector has boomed—ad spending for classifieds alone reached $2.5B in the US and $20.5B worldwide in 2022—and of course, bad bots swarm like bees to honey.

Credential stuffing is a common problem for classified ads websites. This type of attack involves the use of stolen credentials (usernames, passwords, etc.) to try to login to other sites. The credentials are usually obtained by a massive data breach, where the stolen data is either published or sold. Bots make credential stuffing attacks more effective by making login attempts to appear as if they come from many different IP addresses.

Scraper bots steal listings generated on classifieds websites. Unscrupulous businesses can then add the stolen listings to their own websites, even without end-user consent. The victim's classified portal loses out on genuine unique visitors, which dilutes brand value and hurts revenue streams.

Classifieds accounts and forms can be susceptible to **fake account creation and spamming**. For example, the auction website Interencheres.com detected that malicious bots were targeting a form that allows users to request price estimates for their objects. The bots generated up to 14,000 emails per day—which made it impossible to identify authentic requests.

Online bidding and auction sites are also targeted by **sniper and shill bidding bots**, which submit automated bids. Sniper bots submit a bid at the last possible instant to get the lowest price possible. This disrupts the natural bidding process, which leads to lower revenues for auction houses. Shill bots, on the other hand, are used by dishonest sellers to inflate the price of an item via bot-driven bidding. This makes it less likely that genuine users can purchase listed products at a reasonable price.

For any classifieds site, a fast, efficient, and reliable user experience is critical. However, the volume of bad bot activity has grown to enormous proportions, which can negatively affect website performance and consume valuable human resources. For instance, research shows that brute force bot attacks can reach up to 30,000 malicious requests in 10 minutes. Besides putting account data at risk, this kind of activity slows site performance and increases hosting and maintenance costs.

Media

Media sites have struggled with **content theft** since the dawn of the internet.

Content aggregators scrape and repurpose media content in order to generate traffic and advertising revenue for themselves, without doing any of the writing and editorial work. Media monitoring service providers also scrape editorial content in order to use it in the tools and reports they sell, typically without any retribution to authors or publishers.

CASE STUDY

COMBATING CONTENT THEFT

LV Digital GmbH, a company that operates digital products and platforms for the agricultural sector, was heavily impacted by scraper bots targeting their main classified ads portal, Traktorpool. These bots would steal content, repost it on other websites, and significantly drive up infrastructure costs due to increased server load. The constant threat of content theft not only diminished the value of their proprietary listings but also led to misleading analytics and higher operational expenses.

The company struggled with maintaining uptime and ensuring data integrity while combating these aggressive scraping activities. Their in-house measures proved insufficient against the increasingly sophisticated scraping tactics employed by cybercriminals, who often used botnets to launch large-scale scraping attacks. LV Digital realized that combating these scrapers required a more robust and scalable solution.

DataDome provided the necessary bot protection by using advanced machine learning algorithms to detect and block scraper bots in real-time. This solution significantly reduced the server load and protected the integrity of LV Digital's listings. By blocking malicious bots, DataDome ensured that only legitimate traffic reached the site, which also helped in providing accurate data analytics and better resource allocation.

An additional benefit was the improved transparency with data partners, as DataDome's solution ensured that LV Digital did not incur costs for fraudulent traffic. This protection not only saved LV Digital considerable operational expenses but also preserved the company's reputation and the trust of its users and partners.

Today, AI tools like ChatGPT—which typically obtain their training data through scraping—are raising additional ethical issues. As users get answers directly from ChatGPT, they are less likely to navigate to the original source (i.e. the website the data was taken from). Therefore, having ChatGPT serve up information taken from your media website to its users decreases the volume of visitors your pages would have gotten otherwise.

Furthermore, online media platforms are increasingly facing sophisticated bots that manipulate online metrics and public opinions, causing adverse effects. These bots boost engagement metrics like views, likes, shares, and comments across digital channels, in what's known as **Influence Fraud**. This problem spans from political elections to major brand campaigns.

Other Industries

Of course, the list of impacted industries doesn't stop here. While we can't cover them all, here are some additional examples:

Educational institutions and online learning platforms collect immense volumes of proprietary information, making them attractive targets for bot attackers. Attempts may range from scraping course content and research findings to unauthorized access to student data.

The rapidly growing **gaming** industry, with its competitive nature and vast user base, is increasingly vulnerable to bot-driven attacks. Cheating, account takeovers, and in-game fraud are all too common in the gaming world.

The **healthcare industry** faces heavy cyberattacks on an almost continuous basis. This has resulted in the highest average number of exposed databases when compared to other major industries. Hackers like to extort healthcare organizations because, when something malfunctions, even something as simple as email, it puts people's lives at risk. This places enormous pressure on the healthcare organization to give in to the hackers' demands. Consequences of data breaches in the healthcare sector may include loss of productivity, loss of reputation, regulatory penalties, and even potentially the loss of lives.

Effects of Bots on Different Personas

In the digital world, bots do not discriminate. A wide variety of personas are susceptible to the impact of malicious bot activity, with consequences ranging from inconvenience to severe distress.

CASE STUDY

FILTERING INVALID TRAFFIC & SECURING CONTENT

RealClearPolitics (RCP), a leading political news website and polling data aggregator, faced significant challenges due to a rise in invalid traffic (IVT) driven by malicious bots. These bots were responsible for generating fraudulent clicks, page views, and interactions, which not only distorted site analytics but also put a strain on server resources, resulting in slower performance and a degraded user experience for legitimate visitors.

The influx of bot traffic compromised the accuracy of RCP's audience data, which is crucial for understanding reader engagement and for making informed decisions about content and advertising strategies. This distorted data made it difficult for the company to effectively measure user engagement and determine the true value of their advertising inventory. Additionally, the high volume of bot traffic increased the operational costs associated with managing and securing the site.

To address these issues, RCP adopted a bot management solution designed to filter out invalid traffic and protect the integrity of their data. While the focus was on mitigating the immediate impact of bot traffic, the solution also helped safeguard the site's reputation and ensured a smoother, more reliable experience for genuine users.

This case highlights the broader implications of bot traffic for digital media and underscores the importance of employing advanced solutions, like those offered by DataDome, to maintain data accuracy and protect digital assets.

GAMBLING & MEDIA LEAD THE PACK IN PROTECTION

According to DataDome's 2024 Global Bot Security Report, the level of preparedness for bot attacks varies significantly between different industries. The least-protected industries were Health and Luxury, with 70.44% of health domains and 70% of luxury domains failing to detect any of bots used for testing. E-commerce Pure Players, which refers to companies that do not have any retail locations, are also 69.29% unprotected—a shocking statistic, considering all revenue for these businesses comes from online sales.

The industries with the highest levels of bot attack preparedness according to our data were gambling and media. 15.48% of the gambling domains that were tested successfully blocked all the test bots, and 40.48% were protected against at least some bots. And while only 5.56% of media domains blocked all requests, a solid 46.30% successfully blocked some of the test bots.

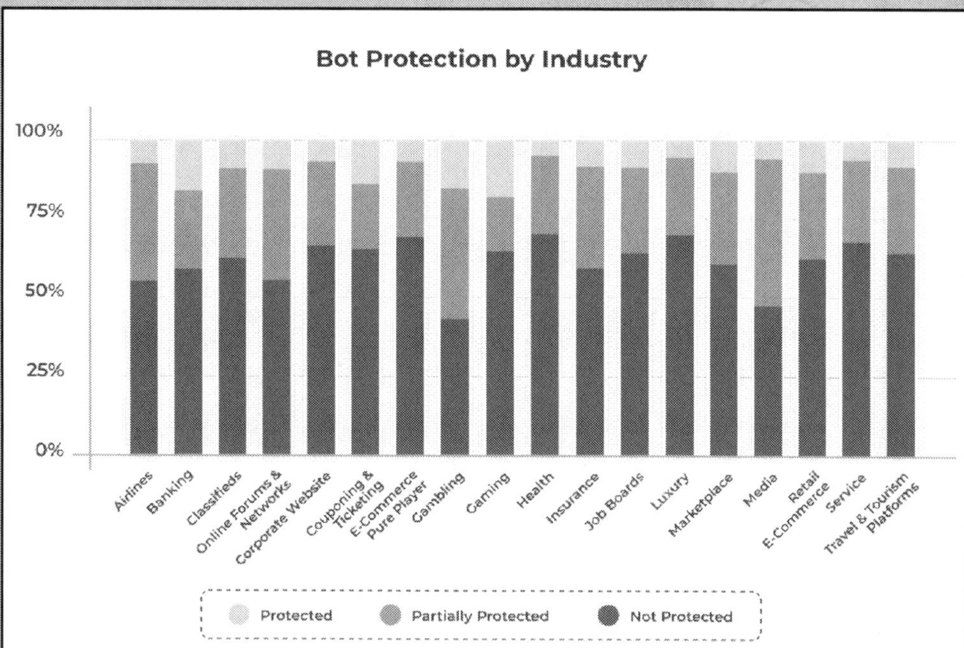

Business Owners & Executives

For business owners and executives in any industry, bot-driven cyberattacks can have devastating consequences. Bots can lead to intellectual property theft, data breaches, and reputational damage that may cause significant financial loss, hinder growth, or even lead to a company's collapse. In some cases, executives may lose their jobs or face legal liabilities in the wake of a severe bot attack.

For instance, in the case of the 2013 data breach at Target that was caused by malware, the CEO resigned, and the company paid approximately $162 million in breach-related expenses, highlighting the severe consequences that business decision-makers can face when they don't prioritize cybersecurity.

Customer Service Representatives

Customer service representatives are often an organization's frontline when it comes to addressing the customer-facing repercussions of bot-driven attacks. Account takeovers, fraudulent transactions, or compromised data can cause irate customers to flood the helpdesk. This puts immense pressure on customer service teams, who must handle complex situations, provide immediate solutions, and maintain the trust of customers in the company.

Cybersecurity & IT Professionals

Cybersecurity and IT professionals bear the hefty responsibility of safeguarding an organization's digital assets against bot attacks. Beyond their everyday responsibilities, IT teams must stay ahead of rapidly evolving bot technologies and craft innovative and comprehensive cybersecurity solutions. Prolonged exposure to the high-stress task of battling bots can result in negative consequences for IT professionals, such as exhaustion, burnout, and high turnover rates within the department.

Developers & Content Creators

Developers and content creators often face challenges from bots that scrape and steal their intellectual property or manipulate the online market for their creations. This results in revenue loss and diminished motivation to produce new content.

The rise of generative AI tools, such as ChatGPT, has added complexity to content theft. These tools scrape the web for content, and your website is no exception, posing risks to copyright protections, data privacy, competitive positioning, and intellectual property rights. Traditional security measures struggle to detect and counteract LLM-driven content scraping, particularly distinguishing between benign and malicious activities. Malicious LLMs can rapidly collect vast amounts of data, devaluing proprietary content and empowering competitors or bad actors with quick access to data and market trends.

Marketing Professionals

Ad fraud is a common problem for marketers. Your ads are clicked by bots instead of your targeted audience. These fake clicks are a complete waste of your advertising budget. They also skew the analytics you rely on to make data-driven decisions. And they can lead to time-consuming clawback arguments with your ad network.

As we've seen, each industry faces its own set of challenges when it comes to bot management and fraud prevention. From ticketing to travel, e-commerce to insurance, and online marketplaces, the impacts of bot activity and fraudulent behavior are both diverse and significant.

While comprehending the unique challenges and solutions is crucial, it is equally important to recognize the broader financial implications of these bot attacks. In the next chapter, we will take a closer look at the costs of unwanted bot traffic, exploring the various ways bot attacks can drain resources and cause substantial financial harm to businesses across all industries.

CHAPTER 6: THE COST OF BOTS

In 2019, Aberdeen Research estimated the annualized risk of bad bots to be **between 2% and 10% of website revenue**, with a median of about 5.6%.

Does this sound exaggerated? We don't think so. In fact, we believe that for many businesses, the real cost of bad bot traffic is even higher.

Malicious bots can directly affect your bottom line in multiple ways. Sometimes, the financial impact of a bot attack is obvious. Very often, however, the costs of bad bot activity are subtle and insidious. As a result, many companies never notice how bad bots are silently siphoning away significant amounts of money.

In this chapter, we put the spotlight on the 15 most predominant such hidden costs, which fall in three broad categories:

- Revenue loss.
- Inflated operational expenses.
- Regulatory penalties.

Website Downtime

For businesses that depend heavily on websites and apps to generate revenue, downtime quickly becomes very costly.

Most people, when they hear of DDoS attacks, will think of so-called volumetric attacks where hackers try to crash the system simply by saturating the bandwidth of the target.

By contrast, Layer 7 (application layer) attacks typically target resource-hungry elements of an application or service, such as a login page or a server executing WordPress. Compared to network layer attacks, Layer 7 DDoS attacks are typically low and slow, but they can be just as disruptive.

Layer 7 DDoS can even happen unintentionally. A leading website for cycling news had so much scraper bot traffic that the site would go down during major cycling events. The bots didn't intentionally take down the website (in fact, downtime made the coveted content unavailable to them, too), but because they came in such large numbers, it happened nonetheless. And many small website owners have learned of unintentional DoS the hard way after a link to their site has been posted to the Reddit front page—an event known as the "Reddit Kiss of Death".

How much would it cost your business if your website or mobile app went down for 15 minutes, an hour, half a day?

To calculate your downtime loss, divide your total annual online revenue by the number of minutes in a year (525,600) and multiply by the number of downtime minutes:

Downtime loss ($) = Annual revenue/525,600 X Downtime minutes

Of course, this calculation only takes into account the direct loss of sales. The time your teams spend fixing the issue, the damage to your brand perception, and other indirect costs will drive the number further up.

Poor Site Performance

In e-commerce, milliseconds matter. And even if unwanted bot traffic doesn't bring your site completely to its knees, it can significantly slow it down, frustrating your legitimate visitors and driving them away.

CASE STUDY

OPTIMIZING WEBSITE SECURITY & PERFORMANCE

Helly Hansen, a leading e-commerce business, faced significant challenges with scraper bots and increasingly sophisticated DDoS attacks. These attacks consumed substantial time and resources, detracting from business-critical operations. The digital development team, supported by Fastly and Magento, was effective at mitigating these attacks but found the process time-consuming and resource-draining.

Helly Hansen's digital development team noted the importance of security and performance for their site experience. The manual effort required to defend against these attacks was unsustainable, pulling focus from other vital operations needed to drive the business forward. The pandemic's acceleration of digital channels only heightened these challenges, making automated bot attack prevention a priority.

The team recognized that attacks were growing more sophisticated and knew they needed a solution that could react faster and more efficiently than their manual methods. They sought an automated approach to preemptively stop attacks and reduce the resource drain on their team.

To address these issues, Helly Hansen implemented DataDome's bot protection solution upon recommendations from their partners, Fastly and Magento. DataDome was chosen for its ease of integration and effective, real-time defense against malicious bot activity. The onboarding process was smooth, and the solution was operational within a week, providing immediate relief.

With DataDome's automated protection, Helly Hansen's team could focus on business growth and innovation without the constant distraction of manual attack mitigation. This proactive approach not only safeguarded the platform but also restored valuable resources to strategic initiatives.

Well over ten years ago, Amazon discovered that even a 100ms increase in website loading time would cost them "substantial and costly drops in revenue". A slow app or website is even worse in today's mobile-first world, as mobile users are even more impatient than desktop users and won't bother if your website takes too long to load.

Poor mobile site performance kills not just traffic, but SEO too: Google factors in page speed for mobile searches.

Bot traffic that deteriorates the performance of your digital assets is an insidious problem, because it's less obvious than a complete takedown. But that makes it all the more important to pay attention to.

According to Kissmetrics, a 1-second delay in page response can result in a **7% reduction** in conversions. If you generate $100,000 per day, this translates to **$2.5 million** in lost sales per year.

Inventory Hoarding

Another indirect way that bots can lose you revenue is by hoarding inventory. This is an insidious and often overlooked type of attack.

Unlike scalper bots, which buy limited-edition items such as event tickets in bulk and resell them with a markup, inventory hoarding bots never actually complete a purchase. Instead, they keep adding products to the shopping cart without ever checking out. Your inventory gets depleted because of these pending purchases, and actual shoppers will eventually get an "out of stock" message.

Most retailers will have a time limit for how long a product can stay in a cart before it is returned to inventory, but hoarder bots can keep track of when the shopping cart empties and add the items back again and again.

Advanced bots will also attack from a vast number of different IP addresses, which makes it difficult to distinguish them from real buyers—unless you have a bot protection solution that can tell the difference between humans and bots.

Inventory hoarding can be particularly disruptive during large e-commerce events such as Cyber Monday or the end-of-year holidays. If you have stocked up on particular goods for the event, but hoarder bots keep making them unavailable for real buyers, you may get stuck with the inventory once demand dies down and be forced to sell it with lower margins.

You may also lose money on companion purchases that real buyers would have made if only they had been able to access the hoarded items.

Price Undercutting

Bots can also sabotage your bottom line by scraping and then automatically undercutting your prices, leading to loss of revenue as consumers choose cheaper competitors over your offers.

Many e-commerce sites use dynamic pricing methods to capture the most deals possible given a wide range of customer attributes. Scraping bots nullify these pricing strategies, as the bots stalk the sites and consistently undercut the price.

In 2017, reports emerged that Amazon had begun restricting bots from Walmart, which were crawling Amazon's listings "several million times a day"[1] to adjust Walmart's prices in response.

There is also a flourishing price monitoring industry, where companies such as Price2Spy and Minderest are using scraper bots for massive and recurring extraction of pricing information from online shops and marketplaces. This detailed and up-to-date competitive intelligence is then delivered to their customers, who can automatically adjust their own listings.

Loss of Reputation

Every year, multiple high-profile data breaches reach the front pages of the news. It's come to the point where we've almost become inured to these data breaches. But each data breach has a significant impact on the company that's affected, and in particular on that company's reputation.

For example, one year after the infamous 2017 Equifax breach, the company had accumulated 36,045 customer complaints and $1.4 billion in costs. Additionally, 46.23% of the Americans who were aware of the breach said that Equifax should have lost or should still lose its ability to act as a credit bureau.

1 https://www.reuters.com/article/technology/amazon-trounces-rivals-in-battle-of-the-shopping-bots-idUSKBN-1860FG/

CASE STUDY

PRESERVING TRUST & CUSTOMER EXPERIENCE

SoundCloud, an audio streaming platform, struggled with fraudulent traffic that undermined user trust and skewed key performance indicators (KPIs). Fake plays, likes, follows, and offensive comments caused significant issues, impacting the platform's recommendation algorithms and business decisions. The engineering team, focused on fostering real interactions between creators and fans, found that managing fraud manually was diverting resources from critical operations and innovation.

SoundCloud initially used in-house models to detect and filter out inauthentic traffic, but these ad hoc measures were insufficient and time-consuming. Fraud became increasingly sophisticated, requiring a scalable and specialized solution. The rise in online traffic and advancements in AI and machine learning further complicated the landscape, necessitating more personnel to keep up, which was not sustainable.

To tackle these challenges, SoundCloud sought an anti-abuse partner capable of accurate, real-time fraud detection across multiple dimensions. After evaluating several vendors, SoundCloud chose DataDome for its precise detection capabilities and cost-effectiveness. During the integration process, DataDome quickly addressed a fraud attack on an endpoint not yet protected, stopping the fraud overnight and proving its effectiveness.

With DataDome's multilayer protection, SoundCloud ensured real user interactions and reliable KPIs, significantly improving the user experience. Creators and fans could trust the platform, resulting in better first-day experiences, increased sign-ups, and fewer offensive comments. This allowed SoundCloud's engineering team to focus on building new functionalities, confident in the accuracy of their data and the security of their platform.

It's a breach of trust that's very difficult to rebuild.

An even more explosive example was the Ashley Madison data breach in 2015. Ashley Madison is an extramarital hookup service; it almost shouldn't need saying that privacy was very important to its users. After the data breach, Ashley Madison's website lost 80% of its traffic. (They also paid $1.6 million to the Federal Trade Commission and $11 million as preliminary settlement for a case on behalf of the 37 million users whose data had been exposed.)

There are countless other examples where bot-driven data breaches caused serious reputational damage and broke trust with consumers around the world.

Wasted Advertising Spend

"Half the money I spend on advertising is wasted; the trouble is I don't know which half." While the 19th-century department store magnate John Wanamaker faced different challenges than today's digital marketers, his everlasting words perfectly summarize the problem of bot-driven ad fraud. How do you know that your digital ads are actually seen by humans, not bots?

Ad fraud is a broad term for the practice of generating fake impressions, page views, clicks, etc. in order to make money off the backs of unsuspecting advertisers. In 2023 alone, ad fraud cost businesses $88 billion dollars—billions spent on fake clicks and bot users, rather than humans.

The mobile app ecosystem is also vulnerable to this threat. In one scheme, uncovered by BuzzFeed News, fraudsters acquired legitimate Android apps and captured the behavior of the app's human users. A vast network of bots was then programmed to mimic this behavior, enabling the fraudsters to bypass inadequate fraud detection systems and steal millions of dollars from advertisers whose ads were shown to bots instead of humans.

In addition to the direct losses, fake traffic to advertising campaigns also skews important metrics. As a consequence, results and insights drawn from the campaign analytics may lead marketers to make wrong decisions for future campaigns.

A Higher CDN Bill

Nearly all major Content Delivery Networks (CDNs) have a pricing model that charges the customer per GB used. Sometimes these prices are publicly available on their websites, sometimes it's an internal calculation that determines a fixed rate with lower and upper bandwidth boundaries.

Bot traffic increases your outbound data transfer volume, and thereby your CDN bill. While a CDN provider might not charge you for the traffic that comes from an obvious cyberattack, not all bot traffic comes in the form of an attack.

Scraper bots, for example, can quietly generate millions of page views that provide no value to you, but that you pay for because of the CDN bandwidth they use. Many new DataDome customers have been astonished to discover that 20, 50 or even 70 percent of their traffic is generated by bots.

A Higher API Bill

Everybody loves APIs. By enabling all kinds of devices and applications to exchange information, via all kinds of communication protocols, APIs help developers create great user experiences much more easily and efficiently.

In order to deliver your digital apps and services, you might be using data and services from multiple third-party providers. Some of these providers may charge a flat monthly subscription fee to access their API, but others may use a metered billing model where you pay for the number of API calls you make.

In the latter case, this means that you also pay for every API call that is generated by a bot. Some bots behave a lot like human users and will generate roughly the same volume of calls, but others are much more intensive and may very quickly rack up your bills.

For example, a human visitor using a store locator might generate a handful of calls to a mapping API, while a bot wanting to scrape every address in the directory could generate hundreds or thousands.

Of course, your own APIs are also vulnerable to abuse if you haven't implemented adequate bot protection. Just like legitimate apps and devices, bots

OVERCOMING SMS TOLL FRAUD

DealStream faced a major challenge when toll fraud incidents began affecting its SMS verification system. Over several weeks, fraudulent bots infiltrated the platform, creating fake accounts and leveraging premium phone numbers for high-cost verification SMS messages and calls.

The team discovered that bots were spamming their SMS verification system so that, when DealStream sent a message or called to check a new user's identity, it was costing a lot. In a short period of time, tens of thousands of SMS messages were sent to premium-rate numbers.

This not only led to considerable financial losses but also strained the platform's resources. Custom code attempts to thwart these attacks proved unsuccessful, so DealStream tried to limit the number of verification attempts for each member. After 10 attempts, the user was deactivated. But this only exacerbated the problem, as the fraudsters started creating even more memberships.

All these fake customers skewed DealStream's statistics and overwhelmed their security staff. A robust solution was urgently needed to preserve DealStream's operational integrity, so the team evaluated multiple providers. DataDome came out on top, as they were impressed by the dashboard and the sophisticated artificial intelligence

With the ability to create custom rules and the assurance that legitimate traffic remains unaffected, the company regained control over its system. The seamless integration of DataDome with the Amazon CloudFront module added an extra layer of efficiency to DealStream's security infrastructure. By using the CloudFront distribution for their website, DealStream ensured a streamlined and optimized connection with DataDome's advanced security features, enhancing the platform's ability to adapt to evolving threats.

will access your APIs to easily find the information they are looking for in the same place and the same format, every time.

If 30% of your third-party API calls are generated by bad bots, how much does it cost you?

Higher Authentication Costs

If any of your online services require authentication with extra security measures, you'll know that there may be costs associated with that.

For example, you may pay for sending out two-factor authentication SMSes whenever a user is logging in.

If such a login page is hit with massive volumes of malicious bot requests, it can generate an SMS bill of tens, if not hundreds, of thousands of dollars in no time.

One global retailer spent approximately $250,000 a month in fraudulent SMS fees before implementing DataDome. Even for a smaller business, an unmitigated credential stuffing attack testing hundreds of thousands of stolen card numbers, for example, could dramatically increase the bill for these CVV2 checks.

Higher Merchant Fees

Merchant fees are the fees charged by a payment service provider (PSP) to a vendor (your business) for processing card transactions. You are charged a percentage of every single transaction through your provider—even if the transaction is fraudulent, or you eventually have to refund the cardholder.

You're also charged for each transaction attempt that goes through the payment processor, even if the payment fails. For example, if bots are testing credit card numbers en masse using small transactions on your website, you will end up paying fees for each test transaction. Considering bots are used to test hundreds or thousands of card numbers in short order, your transaction fees can add up fast.

In addition, if enough chargebacks are filed compared to the number of non-fraudulent transactions, the PSP fees will increase—or the PSP can stop supporting your business entirely.

THE ROI OF REDUCING PAYMENT FRAUD

As an example of the financial benefits you can see by reducing payment fraud and account takeover (ATO) attacks, consider the case study of a global hotel enterprise now protected by DataDome.

In the 90 days prior to activating DataDome protection, the global hotel client had 392,570 credit card declines, even though they had an alternative bot protection software in place.

With enterprises typically being charged an authorization fee between $0.15 and $0.25 per transaction—including declines and voids—the hotel had lost roughly $98,142.50 in declined transaction fees in just one quarter. Had that rate continued, the hotel enterprise would have lost approximately $374,865 in one year to payment fraud alone.

Within the first 90 days after the hotel enterprise replaced their prior bot manager with DataDome, credit card declinations were reduced by 95.5%, saving the client nearly $400,000 over a 12-month period.

The reduction in fraudulent account activity and credit card transaction declinations more than paid for DataDome's solution.

Time Spent Mitigating Bot Traffic & Fraud

This cost is fairly self-explanatory. Managing bot traffic, and in particular bot attacks, takes up the precious time of your IT and/or DevOps teams.

Manual methods for dealing with bots, such as blocking malicious IP addresses, can be extremely time-consuming and are largely ineffective. The same goes for maintaining a WAF; today, bot operators with malicious intents can easily rotate through vast numbers of different IPs, including residential IPs with excellent reputations. At DataDome, we have seen credential stuffing attacks on customer websites coming from 250,000 different IP addresses distributed across more than 8,000 autonomous systems.

Dealing with attacks in incident mode is also costly and bad for morale. A large French retail chain estimated that before installing the DataDome solution, the time spent mitigating bot attacks cost them approximately $9,000 per month.

Furthermore, dealing with bot attacks manually using inadequate tools can lead to errors in production, such as blocking legitimate human traffic by mistake.

OPTIMIZING AD SPEND BY ELIMINATING BOT TRAFFIC

Kelkoo specializes in e-commerce advertising, helping publishers monetize their audience through ads and ensuring that merchants receive quality traffic. Bot traffic inflating their ad spend and distorting analytics. Their in-house detection system, while effective, required continuous updates and the equivalent workload of a full-time engineer to manage evolving bot tactics.

By implementing DataDome's advanced bot detection solution, Kelkoo was able to accurately distinguish between genuine user interactions and fraudulent bot traffic, significantly reducing the incidence of click fraud. This transition allowed Kelkoo to optimize their ad spend, ensuring that their budget was used efficiently for genuine user engagement rather than wasted on bots.

Moreover, using a third-party solution like DataDome provided Kelkoo with neutral, reliable data, which was crucial in negotiations with publishers. This ensured that Kelkoo doesn't pay for automated traffic, leading to more transparent and fair dealings with their advertising partners.

In essence, the substantial cost savings came from eliminating the need for a full-time engineer dedicated to bot management and avoiding unnecessary payments for fraudulent traffic. Kelkoo's engineering team could then focus on enhancing the company's primary services, leading to improved productivity and better allocation of resources. This case underscores the significant hidden costs associated with bot traffic and the value of specialized bot protection solutions in maintaining operational efficiency and financial integrity.

Defrauded Customers

Cybercriminals don't always target you directly. Sometimes, they'll attack your customers through weak links in your system, which can also generate significant costs to you.

Loyalty and reward programs are particularly vulnerable to these types of attacks. The Loyalty Fraud Prevention Association estimates the global value of rewards accounts to approximately $250 billion—but the security of these accounts is often very weak.

Furthermore, consumers generally pay little attention to these accounts, and fraudulent use of rewards may not be discovered until weeks or months later. As a result, loyalty accounts are low-hanging fruit for cybercriminals.

For businesses, the most direct cost related to loyalty program fraud is reimbursements for stolen rewards or fraudulent redemptions. But if your loyalty program is hacked, your business will also face two other types of financial risk: a public relations risk both for the program and for your brand, and the risk of losing disgruntled customers.

Increased Cybersecurity Insurance Premiums

Cyber insurance providers determine premiums based on the associated risk when insuring your business. Organizations that are more vulnerable to bot attacks are viewed as higher risk. This can lead to higher premiums to offset the increased likelihood of claims.

Organizations prone to these attacks may file more frequent claims due to breaches, fraud, or downtime, prompting insurers to raise premiums to cover the anticipated higher volume of claims.

Additionally, bot attacks can cause substantial financial losses, including data breaches, loss of customer trust, and regulatory fines, leading insurers to charge higher premiums to mitigate these financial risks. The resource-intensive nature of responding to bot attacks, coupled with the potential for reputational damage and regulatory compliance issues, further elevates the cost of premiums.

Overall, the heightened risk profile and associated costs compel insurers to adjust premiums accordingly for organizations that are not properly protected against bot attacks.

Personal Data Protection Penalties

Legislators in many countries and states have introduced regulations that intend to protect consumer privacy and data security. The best-known are the General Data Protection Regulation (GDPR) in the European Union and the California Consumer Privacy Act (CCPA).

Both these legal frameworks come with hefty fines for companies that fail to comply. And both regulations apply to you if you collect data from EU or California residents, respectively—regardless of where your business is located.

Bot-driven breaches, such as unmitigated account takeover attacks, will expose you to GDPR penalties up to €20 million, or up to 4% of your annual worldwide turnover of the preceding financial year, whichever is higher.

Regulatory bodies are actively monitoring whether companies are following the rules. In 2020, the UK's Information Commissioner's Office (ICO) fined British Airways £183.39M for exposing the personal data of approximately 500,000 customers.

As for the CCPA, the maximum fine for unintentionally failing to comply is just $2,500, but the act also contains a private right of action for consumers if a business experiences a data breach. These damages may include $100 to $750 per consumer per incident, plus injunctive or declaratory relief and "any other relief the court deems proper".

Having insufficient personal data protection measures could hurt your bottom line indirectly, too. Facebook Dating missed its European launch in time for Valentine's Day 2020, because Ireland's Data Protection Commission raised concerns about its GDPR compliance.

PCI DSS Compliance Penalties

The Payment Card Industry Data Security Standard (PCI DSS) is a data security standard for businesses that handle card payments. Payment card data is often the primary target in attacks against e-commerce sites: by obtaining the primary account number (PAN) and other sensitive authentication data, cybercriminals can impersonate the cardholder and use the card for fraudulent transactions.

The 12 PCI DSS requirements include an obligation to protect cardholder data, and to address new threats and vulnerabilities on an ongoing basis. This is where adequate protection against malicious bots play an important role.

Card cracking, also known as card testing, is a type of threat where malicious bots execute brute force attacks against a payment interface to identify missing values for stolen credit or debit card data, such as the expiration date.

Carding, on the other hand, involves the testing of PAN and its related values against application payment procedures to test the validity of the data. Left unmitigated, both types of attacks will put you at risk of leaking sensitive cardholder data.

Penalties for PCI compliance violations are not widely publicized, and they depend on factors such as the number of yearly transactions processed, the number of months spent in non-compliance, and whether or not it is the first violation. But generally speaking, fines may range from $5,000 to $100,000 per month.

If a data breach occurs as a result of insufficient implementation of the standard, you may also be fined up to $500,000 per security breach plus various compensation costs. Finally, credit card companies may revoke your right to process credit card transactions, which would mean a death sentence for most online businesses.

The negative financial impacts of malicious bot traffic and online fraud attacks can range from immediate to delayed, and be both severe and long-lasting. That's why most enterprise leaders will tell you that finding the right bot protection will save you money in the long run, from averted costly attacks to employee hours saved from manual bot mitigation.

CHAPTER 7: WHY BOTS BYPASS TRADITIONAL DEFENSES

Bot mitigation is the process of using software, solutions, and systems to detect, manage, and block bots and their traffic. The primary goal of bot mitigation is to distinguish between good and bad bots, allowing the former to operate while stopping the latter in their tracks.

Traditional bot mitigation strategies include tools and techniques such as CAPTCHA challenges, IP blocking, and rate limiting to identify and stop harmful bots without affecting the user experience for legitimate visitors.

In today's landscape, however, these traditional defenses against bots and online fraud are increasingly proving inadequate. In this chapter, we look at the inherent limitations of the most common security measures and the pressing need for more advanced, adaptive solutions.

Why is bot detection so challenging?

First, bots now attack all endpoints. They no longer target just websites. They also attack mobile apps, web apps, servers, and APIs. Leaving any endpoint unprotected is dangerous, so simple website bot detection isn't enough.

Second, bots now use the same technologies as humans. They use browsers that have extremely similar fingerprints to human browsers. They can also, for example, resort to mobile phone farms to use real devices instead of simulated ones.

Third, bot operators can easily distribute their attacks across time and space. They can attack your mobile app API for several days across a wide variety of countries, all with little effort and for little money.

Fourth, bots can rotate through millions of clean, residential IPs. Often, each IP will send no more than one or two requests before the bot switches to another IP. Many security solutions, such as WAFs, rely exclusively on IPs to distinguish bots from humans. This trick renders them ineffective.

Fifth, the emergence of bots as a service (BaaS) means anyone can launch a bot attack. BaaS give malicious operators the ability to set up a botnet and send bots to your website or app. Because the services are set up, so users only pay for successful requests, BaaS providers are incentivized to make their bots as advanced as possible.

Recognizing Signs of Bad Bot Activity

Detecting the presence of bots and fraudulent activities begins with recognizing subtle signs that can indicate a breach in digital defenses. Indicators that something bad is happening on your websites, apps, and APIs include:

Abnormally high pageviews. Certain bot attacks will try to overwhelm your servers. Whether it's a DDoS attack or a large number of scrapers, you might see a sudden, inexplicable pageview spike in your analytics software.

Abnormally high bounce rate. Every bot has a goal. Once it achieves its goal or realizes it cannot achieve its goal, it will leave immediately. Because bots operate in milliseconds instead of seconds, you might see an abnormally high and fast bounce rate.

Abnormal session durations. Sessions in the range of milliseconds are suspicious, as are abnormally long sessions. Humans tend to stay for at least a few seconds, but don't often stay on one page for more than a few minutes. Keep an eye out for session duration outliers in your analytics software.

Spikes in traffic from unexpected locations. For example, if your business doesn't operate in Vietnam, but you suddenly receive an influx of requests

NEARLY 2 IN 3 DOMAINS UNPROTECTED AGAINST SIMPLE BOT ATTACKS

For its 2024 Global Bot Security Report, DataDome tested 14,303 of the largest global transactional websites for bot attack preparedness. Each website was subjected to three distinct types of bot requests—all common, basic bot attack vectors that effective bot protection solutions should easily detect.

Of all the domains that were tested, only 8.44% were fully protected and successfully blocked all requests from the test bots. 26.4% were partially protected, detecting and blocking some of the bots, but not all. And a staggering 65.2%— nearly 2 out of 3 businesses—were completely unprotected, letting through all different types of bot attacks.

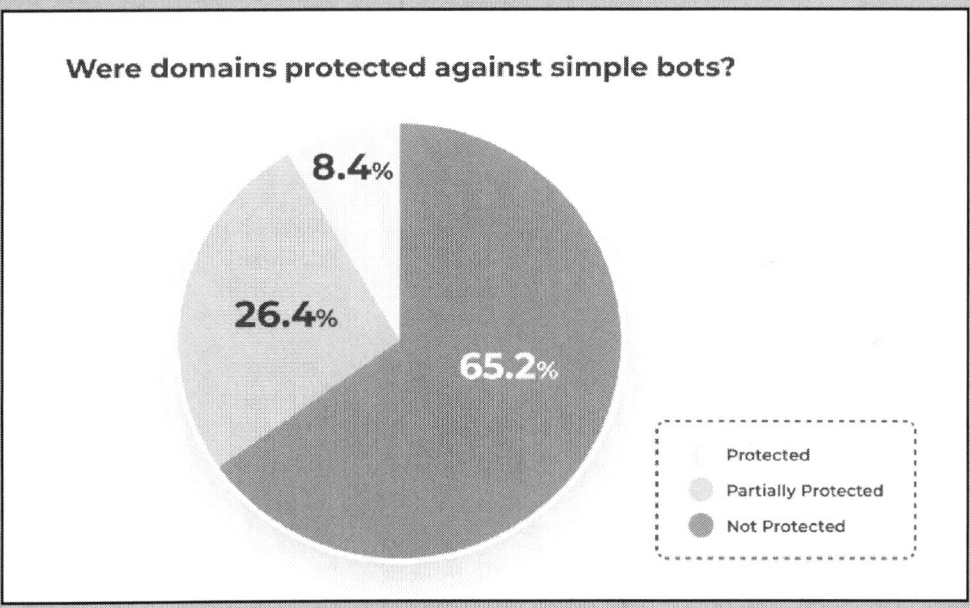

The DataDome BotTester tool was designed to enable a simple assessment of any website's resilience against the most common, basic bot attacks. But as the online threat landscape continues to evolve and increase in complexity, the most substantial threats are currently arising from advanced bot attacks.

from that country, there's a good chance it's a bot attack. Requests coming from countries that don't make sense for your business are often bot requests.

Junk conversions. Are you receiving contact form submissions that make no sense? Do certain users constantly place items in their shopping carts without buying them? Does your free newsletter suddenly have a large number of bouncebacks? All these are junk conversions that indicate bot behavior.

Low conversion rates. A noticeable decrease in conversion rates despite consistent traffic can signal bots inflating visitor numbers without genuine engagement.

Abnormal advertising campaign performance. Campaigns experiencing unusually low performance metrics, such as low click-through rates or engagement levels far below industry benchmarks, might be subject to click fraud perpetrated by bots.

Payment anomalies. Elevated payment processor fees or an uptick in chargeback rates can point to fraudulent transactions facilitated by bots, exploiting vulnerabilities in payment processes.

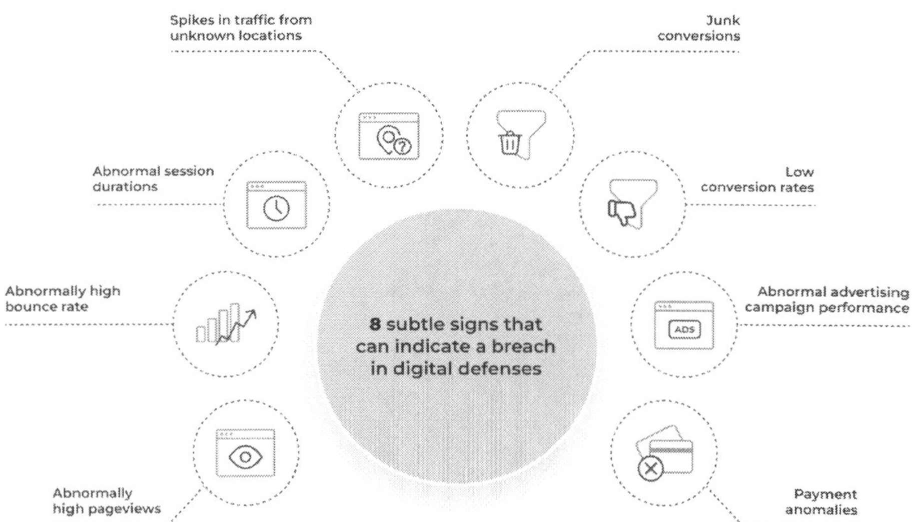

Recognizing signs of bot activity is only the first step, however. The real challenge lies in accurately identifying malicious bot requests and implementing effective mechanisms to block them. Unfortunately, many formerly efficient methods for bot mitigation are no longer adequate.

Rate Limiting

Rate limiting has traditionally been a cornerstone of web security, designed to prevent abuse by capping the number of requests a user can make to a server within a given time frame. By setting thresholds on the rate of incoming traffic, rate limiting aims to mitigate the risk of various attacks, such as brute force login attempts, web scraping, and denial of service (DoS) attacks. However, as bots have become more sophisticated, the effectiveness of rate limiting as a standalone defense mechanism has significantly diminished.

Rate limiting controls the flow of traffic to a server by specifying the maximum number of requests allowed per user within a certain period. This can be implemented in various ways:

- **Fixed Window Limiting**: Limits the number of requests a user can make in a fixed time window.
- **Sliding Window Limiting**: Offers a more dynamic approach by continuously evaluating the request rate within a sliding time window.
- **Token Bucket Limiting**: Allows bursts of requests within a limit, replenishing the allowed request count over time.

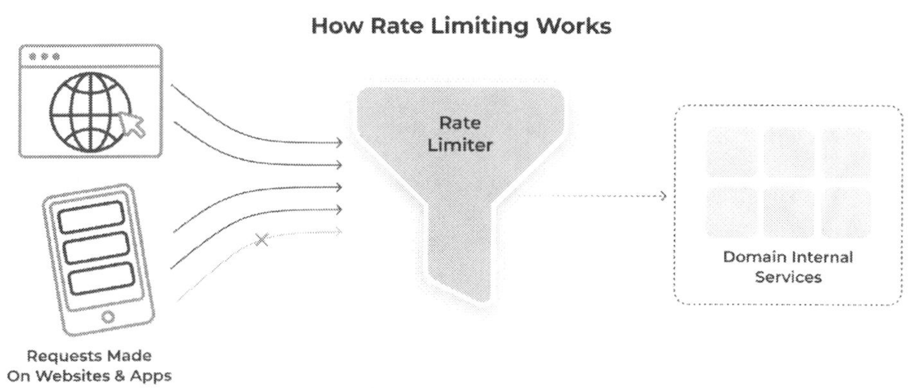

These methods aim to throttle excessive requests, thereby protecting the server from overload and preventing abusive behaviors.

However, modern bots have evolved to exploit the limitations of traditional rate limiting. Several factors contribute to the ineffectiveness of rate limiting against sophisticated bot attacks:

Distributed attacks: Bots now use a technique known as distributed denial of service (DDoS) to bypass rate limiting. By distributing requests across a vast network of bots, often called a botnet, attackers can stay below the threshold set by rate limiting policies. Each bot in the network sends a small number of requests, collectively overwhelming the server without triggering rate limits.

Residential proxies: Bots increasingly use residential proxies to mask their origin and rotate through numerous IP addresses. This approach makes it difficult for rate limiting mechanisms, which often rely on IP-based rules, to detect and block malicious traffic effectively. Residential proxies allow bots to appear as legitimate users from various locations, slipping under the radar of IP-centric rate limiting.

Human-like behavior: Advanced bots can mimic human-like behavior, such as varying the time between requests and simulating mouse movements and typing patterns. This sophistication helps them avoid detection by rate limiting mechanisms designed to identify abnormal traffic patterns.

Rotating user agents: Bots can rotate through different user agents to further obfuscate their identity. By changing user agents frequently, bots can bypass rate limiting mechanisms that track and limit requests based on user agent strings.

Web Application Firewalls (WAFs)

Web application firewalls (WAFs) represent another long-standing pillar of web security. Designed to protect web applications from attacks that attempt to exploit common software vulnerabilities, they analyze incoming traffic, including both GET and POST-based HTTP requests, and apply a set of predefined rules (or "policies") to filter out suspicious traffic that matches familiar attack signatures.

Typically deployed through a reverse proxy or load balancer, WAFs can be cloud-based, host-based, or network-based. They are often IP-centric, blocking traffic from known malicious IP addresses and monitoring user agents classified as undesirable. Common attacks mitigated by WAFs include:

- **Cross-Site Scripting (XSS)**: Attackers inject and execute malicious scripts in another user's browser.
- **Structured Query Language (SQL) Injection**: Attackers access and potentially change sensitive data located in SQL databases.
- **Web Session Hijacking**: Attackers hijack a session ID (normally stored within a cookie or URL) and masquerade as an authorized user.

While WAFs can effectively block known threats and attacks from user agents classified as undesirable, they need to analyze traffic in real-time to block malicious activities.

> "The WAF did a pretty good job of identifying bots, but it has to analyze traffic while it's happening before it can block anything. It takes a few minutes for it to kick in, so we were still having this situation where multiple times per week, we'd be down for 5 minutes."
>
> Will Brown, President of eTool Developers

How Bots Have Outgrown WAFs

Bots have been improving in their ability to sneak past your WAF in more ways than one, thanks to increases in both the quality (ability to appear human and pass security checks) and quantity (availability of bots as a service and distribution of proxies) of resources used by attackers.

Quality of Bots: Bot developers continuously improve the sophistication of their tools. Modern bots use advanced techniques to forge fingerprints and bypass CAPTCHAs, including headless browsers and tools like Puppeteer Extra Stealth.

Quantity of Bots: The sheer number of bots has surged, with almost half of online traffic today composed of bots. The availability of bots as a service (BaaS) has made it easier and cheaper for fraudsters to access high-quality, sophisticated bots.

As mentioned, WAFs analyze incoming GET and POST-based HTTP requests and apply predefined rules to filter out suspicious traffic with familiar attack signatures. However, many advanced bots do not carry attack signatures or target software vulnerabilities. Instead, they exploit the limitations of WAFs by using sophisticated techniques such as:

- **AI-Based CAPTCHA Solving**: Bots use AI tools to solve CAPTCHA challenges even more quickly and accurately, rendering this defense ineffective.
- **TLS Fingerprint Spoofing**: Bots manipulate low-level signals, like Transport Layer Security (TLS) fingerprints, to evade detection.
- **IP Rotation**: Bots use residential proxies to rotate through a vast pool of IP addresses, making IP-based rate limiting and geoblocking ineffective.
- **Human-Like Behavior**: Bots mimic legitimate user behavior, such as mouse movements and typing speed, to avoid detection.

These capabilities allow bots to bypass tools which rely heavily on static rules and IP reputation.

Content Delivery Networks (CDNs)

Content Delivery Networks (CDNs) have become essential for enhancing website performance and security by distributing content across multiple servers globally. However, their effectiveness in bot management and online fraud prevention is limited.

The Limitations of CDNs in Bot Management

While CDNs offer benefits such as caching, load balancing, and DDoS protection, they are not specifically designed to handle advanced bot mitigation. CDNs typically lack the sophisticated analysis tools and real-time threat intelligence required for effective bot management. Comprehensive bot mitigation involves advanced behavioral analysis, machine learning models, and up-to-date threat data, all of which are beyond the typical scope of CDN services.

Most of the strategies that enable sophisticated bots to bypass WAFs also limit the effectiveness of CDSs. By sending low volumes of traffic at high frequency, they can evade rate-limiting rules, while headless browsers and AI-driven techniques enable them to mimic human behavior.

Enhancing CDNs With Bot Management Solutions

Integrating specialized bot management solutions with CDNs can address their limitations. These solutions provide advanced behavioral analysis using machine learning algorithms to detect bot activity based on user behavior. Real-time threat intelligence helps block known malicious actors, while multi-layered authentication adds additional user verification steps to challenge and identify bots. Device fingerprinting creates unique identifiers for devices, allowing for more accurate detection and blocking of bots based on their configurations.

Combining CDNs with advanced bot management solutions creates a robust defense against sophisticated bot attacks, protecting digital assets and online users more effectively. This integration is essential for organizations aiming to safeguard their web applications against the evolving threat landscape posed by modern bots.

Can't CAPTCHA 'em All

Traditional CAPTCHAs (like reCAPTCHA) were created in the late 1990s to prevent bots from spamming search engines or forums. Bots weren't so hard to filter out back then, and gen 1 CAPTCHAs worked reasonably well for almost two decades.

That being said, the impact of a CAPTCHA on human users should not be underestimated. Ever since their inception in 1997, CAPTCHAs have been criticized for making the web more inaccessible. They make the user experience worse for all users, particularly for users with disabilities, who may struggle with text, audio, or image recognition challenges.

Furthermore, the landscape has shifted, and traditional CAPTCHAs no longer efficiently stop bots. According to DataDome's research, 50% of "users" that pass Google's reCAPTCHA are bots.

What are CAPTCHA bots?

A CAPTCHA bot is a computer program that is used to automatically complete CAPTCHAs. Hackers and cybercriminals use CAPTCHA bots to automatically access forums, registration pages, login pages, and other places that companies attempt to secure with a CAPTCHA.

The least sophisticated CAPTCHA bots will use a brute force attack to guess the correct answer to a CAPTCHA challenge. This involves rapidly trying every possible combination of letters and numbers until the bot finds the correct answer.

Other bots send their challenge to a CAPTCHA farm, a service where a pool of human workers (usually in developing countries) solve CAPTCHAs all day for very little money. When a bot is blocked by a CAPTCHA challenge, it makes an API call to the CAPTCHA farm with the website's CAPTCHA public key and domain name as parameters. In less than a minute, the challenge is solved by one of the CAPTCHA farm workers, and the bot obtains its response token. The bot then passes the CAPTCHA challenge by submitting the response token.

Some CAPTCHA bots are more sophisticated and use Optical Character Recognition (OCR) to read and solve the CAPTCHA challenge. Additionally, image and text recognition AI is increasingly available and now sophisticated enough to be added to malicious CAPTCHA bots.

In summary, the rule of thumb is that CAPTCHAs can never be your only line of defense. On their own, they stand little chance of effectively stopping bots. CAPTCHAs are only valuable if they are part of a comprehensive bot defense strategy.

In-House Bot Protection Solutions

When defenses like CAPTCHAs and WAFs fall short against bot attacks, some organizations attempt to build their own in-house bot protection solutions. These "homegrown" approaches are tailored specifically to the unique needs and infrastructure of the organization, but they come with their own set of challenges and limitations.

What are in-house bot protection solutions?

In-house bot protection solutions are custom-developed systems designed to detect and mitigate bot traffic within an organization's specific environment. These solutions often incorporate a variety of techniques, such as:

- **Custom Rate Limiting**: Implementing bespoke rate limiting strategies tailored to the typical traffic patterns of the organization's applications.
- **Behavioral Analysis**: Developing algorithms to analyze user behavior and identify anomalies that might indicate bot activity.
- **IP deny and allow listing**: Maintaining internal lists of known malicious IP addresses to block, and trusted IP addresses to allow.
- **Device Fingerprinting**: Creating unique identifiers for devices based on their configuration and behavior to detect and block bots.
- **Honeypots**: Setting up hidden traps that only bots would interact with, helping to identify automated traffic.

Advantages & Limitations of In-House Solutions

In-house bot protection solutions offer several advantages. First, they provide a high degree of customization, allowing organizations to tailor the defenses specifically to their unique traffic patterns and needs, which can enhance detection effectiveness. Second, these solutions offer full control over implementation, enabling quick adjustments and fine-tuning as new threats emerge. Third, in-house solutions can seamlessly integrate with existing systems and workflows, potentially strengthening the overall security posture.

However, there are also significant challenges. Developing an effective in-house system is resource-intensive, requiring substantial investments in skilled personnel, time, and ongoing financial support. Many organizations also lack the specialized knowledge needed to stay ahead of the rapidly evolving bot threat landscape, which can hinder the effectiveness of their defenses.

Scalability is another concern, as custom solutions may struggle to handle increasing traffic volumes and the growing sophistication of bot attacks. Additionally, in-house teams may experience delays in responding to new and emerging threats compared to dedicated third-party solutions that are designed for rapid updates and adaptability.

Finally, the ongoing maintenance and updates required to keep the solution effective can be complex and time-consuming, further straining resources.

The shortcomings of traditional defenses against bots and online fraud illustrate the need for more advanced cybersecurity strategies. By understanding the limitations of existing defenses and adopting proactive measures, businesses can safeguard their digital assets, protect customer trust, and mitigate fraud risk.

CHAPTER 8: MANAGING BOTS & KEY CRITERIA FOR EFFECTIVE BOT PROTECTION

The current state of bot development presents multiple challenges to protective measures:

- Bots have access to tools that enable them to have a near-perfect fingerprint. They can easily forge low-level signals, such as TLS fingerprints.
- Bots have access to millions of residential proxy IPs located all around the world. These residential proxies enable them to bypass traditional detection mechanisms such as IP-based rate limiting and geoblocking.
- Traditional CAPTCHAs—whose security rely solely on the difficulty of the challenge—have become ineffective against bots.
- The latest AI progress in audio and image recognition techniques significantly speeds up the time and monetary cost for bots to solve CAPTCHAs.

Given these challenges, what then defines truly state-of-the-art bot detection today?

To effectively combat sophisticated bot attacks, two primary objectives are essential:

- **Discovering previously unknown bot patterns**: This involves identifying new and emerging threats that traditional detection methods might miss.
- **Blocking malicious traffic in real time**: Ensuring that harmful traffic is intercepted instantly to prevent any potential damage.

Server-Side and Client-Side Signals

Bots are evolving by the second, so detection must rely on a variety of signals from many sources to root out malicious actors. Both server-side and client-side signal collection are required for efficient and effective bot detection.

Server-side detection is great for simple bots with suspicious HTTP and TLS (Transport Layer Security) fingerprints, but to identify today's sophisticated bots, more signals are required. Client-side detection helps with browser, app, and user event tracking to detect advanced bots that masquerade more effectively as humans.

Some bot management tools on the market are limited to either client-side or server-side detection, and some only gather very limited signals from one side or the other. The key is to make sure you have options (both client-side and server-side data) to maximize effectiveness and meet future needs.

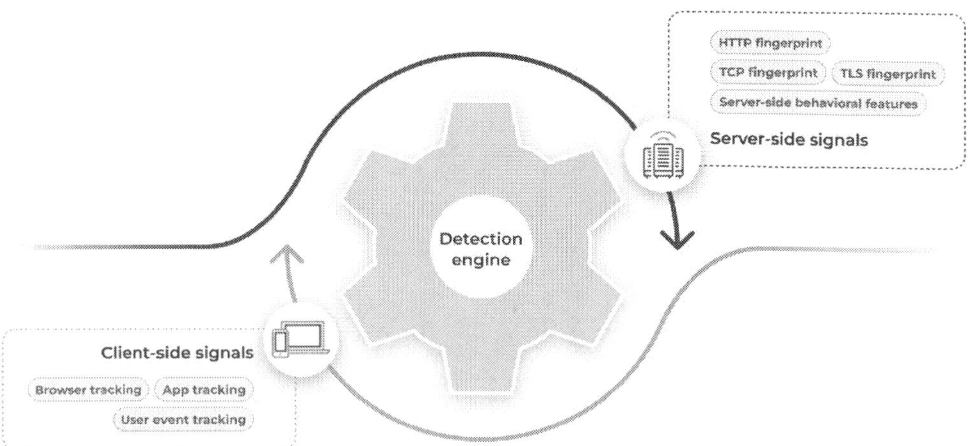

Types of Signals Used in Bot Detection

Advanced bot detection specialists gather and enrich thousands of client-side and server-side signals. This comprehensive data collection allows for both immediate inspection and long-term analysis. The signals fall into three main categories:

Signatures/Fingerprints: These include known patterns of malicious activity, such as specific sequences in HTTP headers or known vulnerability scans. They are effective in identifying threats that match previously recognized attack patterns. This method leverages both server-side and client-side approaches:

- **Server-Side Signatures/Fingerprints**: Based on HTTP headers and TLS fingerprints to identify and block malicious activity before it reaches the client.
- **Client-Side Fingerprints**: Using signals collected through JavaScript or SDKs to create unique identifiers for devices, helping in tracking and identifying potentially malicious devices across different sessions and activities.
- **Device & Web Fingerprinting**: Collecting and analyzing information about a device's hardware, software, and network configurations to create a unique identifier or "fingerprint." This helps in tracking and identifying potentially malicious devices across different sessions and activities.

Behavioral: These signals analyze user interactions, such as mouse movements, keyboard strokes, and scrolling behaviors, to distinguish between human and bot activities. This approach helps in identifying anomalies that deviate from typical human behavior.

Reputational: These are based on the historical behavior of IP addresses, devices, and other entities, assessing their likelihood of being malicious based on past actions. By leveraging reputation scores, security systems can preemptively block or scrutinize known bad actors.

Browser/Mobile PoW: Proof-of-Work (PoW) is used to challenge and validate the legitimacy of browser or mobile client requests. PoW involves requiring the client to perform computational tasks, which are easy for legitimate users but resource-intensive for bots.

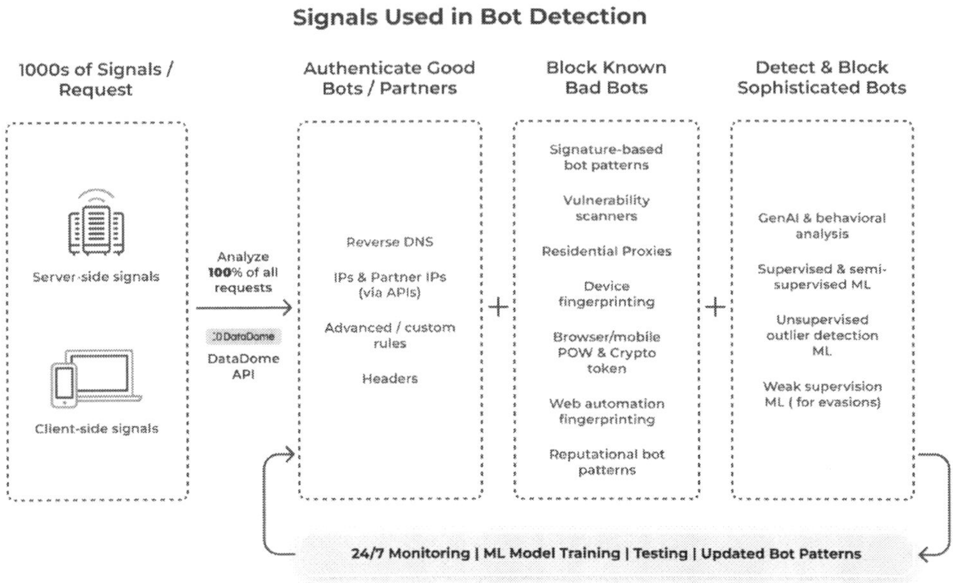

Types of signals collected to detect bots

Real-Time Analysis of Each Request

An effective bot protection solution will scrutinize every request in real time using a combination of the above-mentioned signals. This ensures that no potentially harmful traffic goes unchecked. The comprehensive, real-time analysis of all requests, not just a sample, is crucial for maintaining robust security.

Leveraging AI for Enhanced Detection

AI-powered detection is crucial for interpreting the vast amount of data collected. Machine learning models analyze large datasets to identify patterns, anomalies, and threats with high accuracy. These models improve over time as they learn from historical data, making the AI-powered detection system increasingly effective.

Instead of relying on a single, monolithic model, a layered approach with multiple specialized machine learning models is employed. This means that hundreds of models can run simultaneously, each focusing on different aspects of detection. This layered approach allows for a more nuanced and thorough analysis.

Fingerprints and Session Behavior:

Advanced detection techniques include the use of digital fingerprints and session behavior analysis. Fingerprinting involves collecting data on device attributes, browser configurations, and network information to create a unique identifier for each user. Session behavior analysis examines the user's interactions on the website in real time to detect deviations from normal patterns.

Multi-Layered AI Techniques:

- **Signature-Based Detection**: Uses known patterns and characteristics of malicious bots to identify and block them.
- **Behavioral Analysis**: Evaluates user behavior metrics like mouse movements, scroll patterns, and typing speed to detect anomalies.
- **Time Series Analysis**: Analyzes the timing of user actions and interactions to spot irregularities that are typical of automated bot activities.
- **Fingerprinting**: Collects and analyzes device and browser attributes to create a unique user profile for detecting repeat offenders.
- **Session Analysis**: Tracks and analyzes user session behaviors to identify deviations from typical patterns.

How does AI work in fraud detection?

Because AI is dynamic, it continuously works to reduce the number of false positives (genuine users being blocked) by improving the accuracy of its rules. It does all this at such speeds that it doesn't impact the user experience. The best AI cybersecurity solutions are so lightweight that they won't impact the performance of your website or mobile app either.

Benefits of Using AI in Fraud Detection

- **Real-time detection.** The best AI processes incoming data and blocks new threats in milliseconds.
- **Grows better over time.** The more data you feed the AI, the better its predictions. AI only ever gets better over time, particularly if instances of an AI share knowledge with each other. For example, whenever a DataDome AI instance detects a new threat pattern, it will share it with all other DataDome AI instances globally.

GENETIC ALGORITHMS: USING NATURAL SELECTION TO BLOCK BOT TRAFFIC

Genetic algorithms are an artificial intelligence technique inspired by natural selection. The main structure of a genetic algorithm is as follows:

1. **Initialization**: Create an initial population of potential solutions (individuals).
2. **Evaluation**: Evaluate each individual in the population based on a specific criterion.
3. **Selection**: Select the best individuals from the population to reproduce.
4. **Reproduction**: Combine the genetic material of selected individuals through crossover and create offspring.
5. **Mutation**: Introduce random changes (mutations) in the offspring's genetic material.
6. **Replacement**: Replace the least fit individuals in the population with the new offspring.
7. **Termination**: Repeat steps 2 to 6 until a satisfactory solution is found or a termination condition is met.

The process of selection, reproduction, and mutation mimics natural selection and genetic variation. By introducing randomness and making no assumptions about the nature of the requests to target, genetic algorithms can generate rules to find bot traffic that would not have been detected otherwise.

Initial rules are built by combining predicates (e.g., user agent, country, HTTP method) derived from recent request signatures. A base set of rules can then be created by randomly combining elements from the set of predicates. This base set will serve as the starting point for the algorithm's evolution.

Then, the fitness of each rule—that is, how good the rule is at targeting bot traffic—must be evaluated. This part is challenging; since the goal is to discover bot activity that wasn't detected by any other method, there are no reliable labels to assess if the requests matched by the rule are bot-made or human-made.

One possible approach is to look at the time series of the requests that would have been matched by the rule, and evaluate how similar it is to the time series of known bot patterns (gathered through other detection methods). If a time series presents the characteristics of a bot traffic time series and is different from all known human time series, the associated rule is deemed good and assigned a high score. Otherwise, the rule gets assigned a low score.

Once each rule has been assigned a score, the best-performing rules can be retained ("survival of the fittest") and new rules obtained by combining them—the next generation. Then, random, infrequent mutations are added to the rules in order to introduce new predicates into the population of potential solutions.

For example, a rule can be randomly mutated by removing part of the rule (e.g. Country=France) and replacing it by another key-value from our set of predicates (e.g. ConnectionType=Cellular). Thanks to these random mutations, the algorithm is able to explore new areas of the solution space and potentially find better rules.

The process of scoring potential solutions and combining them into new ones can be repeated over and over, improving the rule population's fitness score with each new generation until enough satisfactory rules have been obtained. The evolution process can then be terminated, and the new rules leveraged in the detection system.

The main benefit of this approach is that it makes no (or very few) assumptions about which parts of traffic to target, or the structure of the output rules. The algorithm explores the space of potential solutions in order to find rules that are gradually better at identifying bot traffic with each new generation.

- **Less time being reactive.** Your employees will spend less time investigating threats and reviewing information thanks to AI for fraud detection. They will have more time for projects that will push your business forward.

Risks of Using AI Fraud Detection

- Social fraud is still a risk. Automated threats aren't the only threats to your company. Phishing, social engineering, and other types of social fraud are hard to combat with AI because such threats aren't automated—and it only takes one employee falling for this type of fraud to compromise the whole company. You will still need to educate your team to fight these risks.
- Black box. Because the AI parses so much data, it can be hard to understand how it actually works. This is particularly true if AI is combined with machine learning and neural networks that simulate a human brain. Still, the best fraud detection software solutions will give you plenty of control to customize its rules.
- False positives. While the best AI for fraud detection software will reduce false positives to a tiny number, it's impossible to eliminate entirely. AI will occasionally block some genuine users, particularly those who use uncommon browsers and VPNs.

Multi-Model Analysis in Real-Time

When a request is received, it can be analyzed in parallel by numerous machine learning models. Some models might focus on detecting anomalies in traffic patterns, while others might evaluate the behavior of the user interaction with the site. If an anomaly is detected, the request undergoes further analysis by additional models to ensure accuracy in determining its nature.

Collective Intelligence & Global Threat Updates

Machine learning models can also leverage collective intelligence, reflecting new threats globally and updating their detection capabilities in real time. Such a global approach ensures that once a threat is identified in one part of the world, the defenses are updated everywhere, providing comprehensive protection against emerging threats.

EXAMPLE: DETECTING CAPTCHA SOLVERS

A specific example of AI in action is the detection of bots masquerading as humans to solve CAPTCHAs. Machine learning models are trained to analyze data from requests and challenges, such as mouse movements, keyboard strokes, and touch inputs. These models use sophisticated techniques to identify non-human behavior accurately, ensuring that bots are effectively detected and blocked.

Incorporating AI into Security Products

Beyond detection, AI capabilities are increasingly being integrated into security products to enhance their functionality. Features such as analyzing suspicious behaviors, prioritizing alerts, and creating custom rules are being enhanced with AI, making these tools more efficient and user-friendly.

Expert Threat Research Teams

Despite the advanced technology, human expertise remains vital. Expert threat research teams play a critical role in staying ahead of attackers. They monitor the latest techniques, participate in underground forums, and analyze anomalies to ensure that defenses are continually updated and effective.

A critical aspect of any successful bot management strategy is the ability to measure its effectiveness and determine which areas need improvement. Identifying the right key performance indicators (KPIs) will help you keep track of your progress, optimize your defenses, and ultimately protect your organization against bot-driven threats and online fraud.

Measuring the Effectiveness of Your Bot Management Solution

Bot Detection Rate

One of the most important KPIs to consider is the bot detection rate. This metric reflects the percentage of bot traffic your management system can successfully identify and flag. A high detection rate indicates that your system is effectively spotting and thwarting potential threats.

False Positive Rate

The false positive and false negative rates serve as essential KPIs when gauging the effectiveness of your bot management strategy. False positives occur when legitimate user traffic is mistakenly flagged as malicious, while false negatives represent bot-driven attacks that slip through undetected. Striking an ideal balance between these KPIs is vital to keeping your organization secure without disrupting the experience for genuine users.

False Positives & Negatives

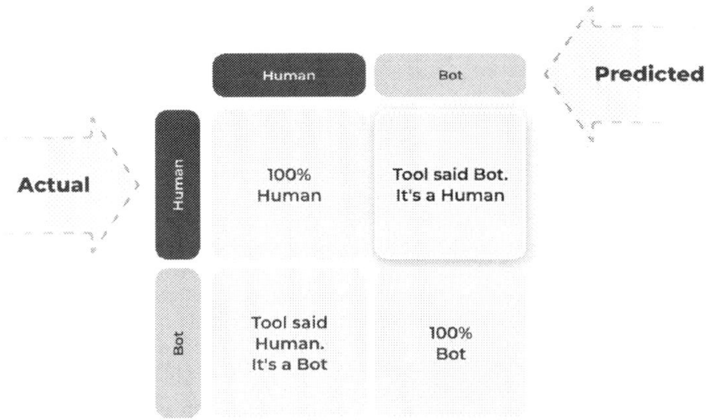

Certain bot management solutions suffer from false positive rates as high as 0.75%, which may not sound high, but is well above the ideal false positive rate of 0.01%. A higher false positive rate adds more friction to your user experience. But dialing back the sensitivity allows sophisticated bots to evade detection. Inaccurate bot detection can also result in many negative consequences beyond a poor user experience and security risks, such as increased fraud costs and reputational damage.

Some bot management vendors claim to have no false positives, but in practice, this is an unrealistic expectation. If a system reports zero false positives, it's almost certain that it's not detecting sophisticated bots effectively, allowing them to slip through undetected. Serious vendors focus on keeping their false positive rate extremely low while recognizing that some level of false positives is inevitable in the pursuit of strong security.

Regular review of these rates will help you pinpoint areas for improvement and inform necessary adjustments for a more efficient and accurate defense.

THE ESSENTIAL ROLE OF SMART FEEDBACK MECHANISMS

To be exceptional at detecting even the most advanced bots, online fraud protection solutions need feedback loops that capture, process and apply new information in real time to constantly improve detection models.

Many bot management solutions will show a CAPTCHA to users with suspicious behavior. The idea is that if the user can solve a CAPTCHA to prove her humanness, the mistake can be taken into account and the algorithm improved. However, as discussed in Chapter 7, solving CAPTCHAs is no longer a real challenge for bots, and the feedback may be misleading.

Other solutions will simply hard block suspicious sessions for a period of time. But with this approach, there is no feedback mechanism at all (other than possibly angry customers on X or TikTok) telling you that the bot detection system has made a mistake. The machine learning model is not... well, learning.

The best solutions will therefore include invisible proof-of-work challenges to complement CAPTCHA. They will also be transparent for customers, providing visibility into key metrics (such as false positive rates) and offering clear explanations for the decisions made by the detection system.

Drawbacks of ML for fraud detection include the potential for false positives, describing when a system mistakenly marks legitimate actions as fraudulent. False positives open up the possibility for a negative feedback loop—if one detection mistake isn't spotted, the algorithm thinks it responded correctly and the behavior was legitimate, teaching itself to repeat the same response in the future.

Thankfully, human insight alongside machine learning can help overcome this problem, which is why 24/7 expert monitoring of all fraud detection machine learning models is recommended.

Response Time

Another crucial KPI to focus on is your bot management system's response time—the time it takes to detect and respond to potential threats or attacks. In the high-stakes realm of cybersecurity, timely responses can mean the difference between a successful defense or a devastating system breach. Monitoring your system's response time ensures that it is capable of reacting swiftly and effectively to known and emerging threats.

HOW DOES BOT TRAFFIC IMPACT LATENCY?

Bot traffic can significantly increase web latency due to the extra requests bots make when loading webpages. Bots are automated programs that crawl websites in order to index content, collect data, or perform other functions. The higher the number of bots crawling through webpages, the more web latency is likely to be experienced by users trying to access those webpages.

For example, if multiple bots request data from web servers at once, they can overload the server and cause some pages to take longer than usual to load. Additionally, malicious bots can send out spam requests, which further add unnecessary strain on web servers and can increase page loading times. By understanding and managing bot traffic, web latency can be reduced significantly, and web performance improved overall.

Remember that not all bot traffic is bad; some bots are helpful in enabling webpages to load quickly and efficiently. Using a bot management solution alongside other security measures such as WAFs can help ensure malicious bot activity is minimized, while allowing beneficial bots to continue their work without adversely impacting web latency.

Additionally, other strategies such as caching data or optimizing web applications for performance can help reduce latency caused by both malicious and benign bot traffic. By reducing web latency resulting from bot requests, webpages will load faster and more reliably for users around the world.

User Experience

User experience is another vital KPI to monitor when evaluating your bot management strategy. Though security measures are essential to safeguard your organization, they can inadvertently create obstacles for loyal customers who may be incorrectly flagged as bots. Understanding the impact of your security measures on end-users can help refine your approach to prevent potential losses due to frustration or inconvenience. By closely monitoring customer feedback, support requests, and dropout rates, you can gain critical insights into areas of improvement and strike the necessary balance between security and convenience.

Other KPIs

Aside from these technical KPIs, consider the impact of your bot management strategy on your organization's overall performance and growth. For instance, have there been reductions in fraud, unauthorized access, or data breaches since implementing your bot management solution? Examining the broader repercussions of your approach—from operational efficiency to reputation—will provide valuable insights into the effectiveness of your bot management efforts.

The complexities of modern bot attacks require an advanced, multi-layered approach to detection and protection. Effective bot management solutions must integrate real-time analytics, machine learning, and adaptable detection models to stay ahead of evolving threats. By evaluating KPIs such as detection rate, false positive rate, and response time, you can continuously refine your defenses and balance security with user experience.

In the next chapter, we'll look beyond technical detection capabilities to explore additional factors that define an enterprise-grade bot management platform. Scalability, ease of deployment, and long-term adaptability are just a few of the key elements that help ensure lasting protection and seamless integration into your organization's digital ecosystem.

CHAPTER 9: SELECTING AN ENTERPRISE-GRADE BOT MANAGEMENT PLATFORM

As a cybersecurity leader, you've likely experienced damaging online fraud attacks—whether in the form of credential stuffing, card cracking, account takeover (ATO), chargeback fraud, or scalping. You are probably aware that fraudsters require automation (bots) to scale and distribute their attacks against businesses like yours.

You might be considering bot protection for one or more reasons:

- Your business leadership is asking you for a fraud prevention plan.
- Key business or operational metrics—ranging from conversion rates and payment decline rates to server overloads and bounce rates—are flashing red.
- You are grappling with the challenge of protecting your business and customers against fraudsters without degrading your user experience.
- Your operations teams are overwhelmed with blocking bots manually.
- You are being asked to move quickly while saving resources on a tight budget.
- You may even have a bot management tool in place, but continue to experience painful recurring symptoms of malicious, fraudulent traffic.

Realizing that your business needs bot protection to reduce your online fraud risk is a vital first step, but there are many bot management tools to choose from. With so many options on the market, how do you determine which solution will best meet your needs?

This chapter will help you make a thoughtful, informed decision by outlining the key capabilities to consider when evaluating different bot management platforms.

Protection Without Compromise

Accuracy is key in bot detection, and so is performance. Interrogating every request every time could cripple many solutions, which is why sampling requests or using token-based techniques are common workarounds. Ask your vendor about the number of points of presence (PoPs) they have in your operating regions and worldwide.

Find out the solution's latency benchmarks for like-for-like detection scenarios. A legacy solution architecture or limited supported PoPs can force you to sacrifice accuracy in order to maintain a smooth user experience for online transactions. Look for a vendor that has the global infrastructure to support your performance requirements and validate that with real-world benchmarks for latency.

For example, here is a map of DataDome's PoPs, with 30+ distributed globally.

DataDome's Point of Presence (PoP) Map

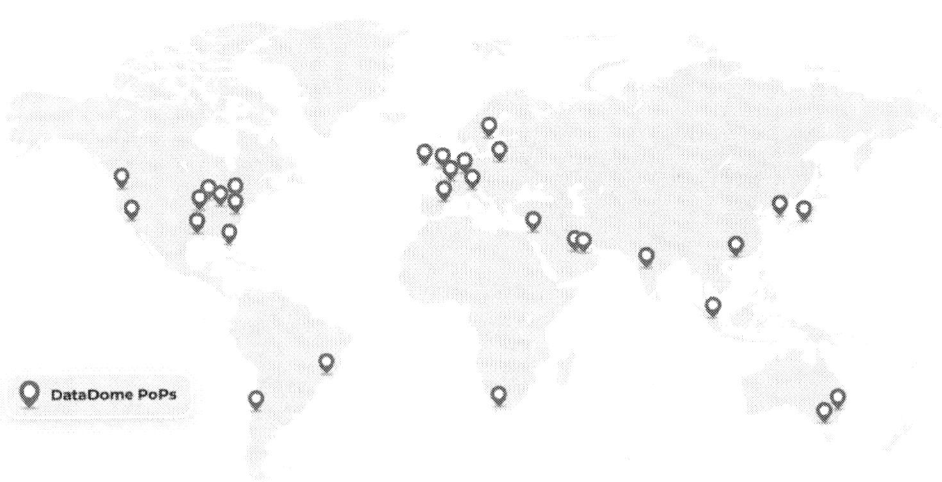

Breadth of Solutions, Use Cases, & Supported Endpoints

Does the vendor only support websites, or do they also protect mobile applications and APIs? Your business must be fully protected consistently to circumvent malicious bots and online fraud.

Is it easy to extend the solution to add new use cases and endpoints to protect? Does the protection leverage both server-side and client-side detection signals—both of which are necessary for securing all endpoints and detecting advanced bots?

Does the vendor offer lightweight SDKs with proof of fast, successful deployment on various devices (iPhone, Android, etc.) and no added latency or impact on the mobile user experience? Will the vendor work to ensure the solution covers each endpoint equally for every use case?

Look for a solution that works on every endpoint, easily scales with your traffic, and can be used to support new use cases when needed.

You may also want to consider a tool that offers discovery capabilities to scan your domain for unprotected endpoints, ensuring all possible points of entry for bots are protected.

End Points That Need Bot Protection

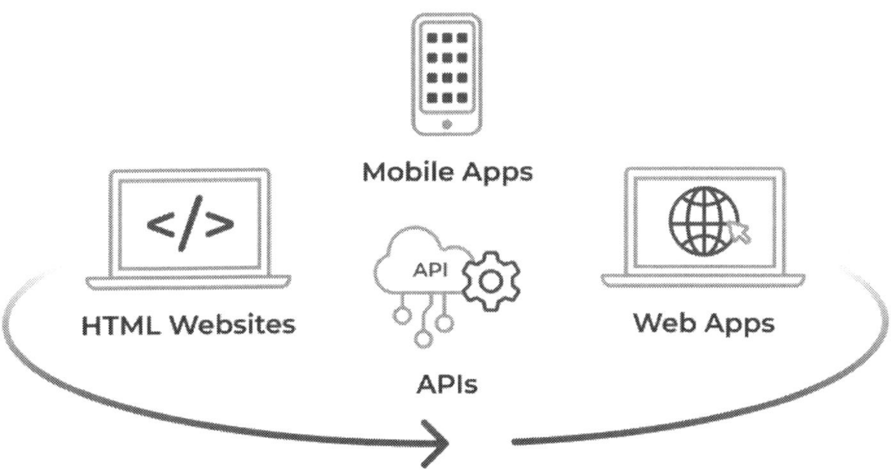

Ease of Implementation & Use

A bot management solution should save you time and resources by protecting you on autopilot. It should run automatically in the background, no matter the volume of bots attempting to attack your infrastructure.

Does the software require a lot of customization to fit into your organization's architecture? Are manual interventions necessary? Does it require continuous tuning from your SecOps team to keep the protection working? How easy to understand and use is the interface?

Look for a solution that can be integrated into your tech stack quickly and easily to ensure quick time to value. You can also look for a vendor that offers the possibility of multiple tenants within one enterprise or business, to allow for better customization to your business' needs. Also, choose a vendor that provides intuitive and easy-to-use dashboards and reporting to keep track of the protection's performance and your ROI.

Reporting & Analytics Capabilities

Being able to get real-time threat information and set the protection you need fast is critical. Avoid sifting through several reports and pages or sitting through weeks of software training to get the information you need.

You should get easy access to a real-time view of all your incoming requests and web traffic, including the threats attacking your website, app, and API—at a glance, as well as different, more detailed views.

Look for the ability to examine specific events, quickly drill into relevant information, and view your traffic by attack type, user, account, trend, and other views that help reveal patterns and useful insights. You may also want to inquire about a mobile app companion to see attack alerts and explore traffic information on the go.

In addition to a user-friendly dashboard, your solution should provide various reports and analytics your team can drill into if needed. The right analytics will help you quickly gain insights from a complex data set.

Custom reporting is an important capability that can allow you to easily generate and share relevant information with key stakeholders across your organization. In contrast, subpar reporting can become time-consuming for your team to support.

Peer Reviews & Industry Recognition

When you evaluate a bot management solution, consider how the provider is viewed by both its customers and industry analysts. Customer feedback offers insight into a provider's performance in real-world scenarios, with key indicators such as detection effectiveness, protection performance, user experience, and support quality. High user ratings and a solid Net Promoter Score (NPS) reflect a positive customer experience and effective support, signaling that the vendor consistently delivers on its promises.

For broader industry insight, reputable sources like the G2 Grid® Report and the Forrester Wave™ report for Bot Management Software provide valuable perspectives.

G2 Grid® Report for Bot Detection and Mitigation Software

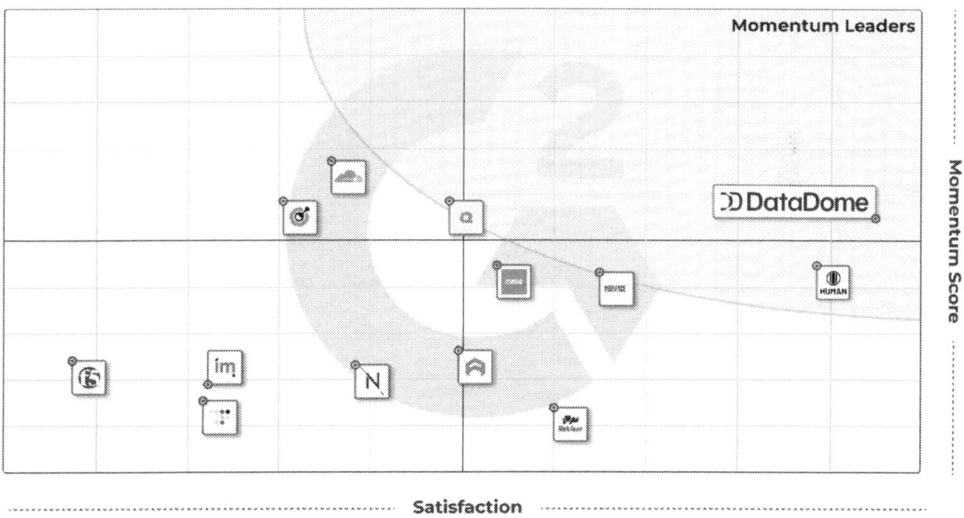

The G2 Grid ranks software solutions based on customer reviews and market presence, helping businesses evaluate and compare solutions within a specific category.

These reports are compiled by organizations with extensive experience and trusted client engagements, enabling a thorough assessment of vendors based on independent criteria.

Implementation Track Record

Another important metric to examine is a vendor's track record of successful implementations. Are customers happy with the product and its ease of onboarding and implementation in their architecture? Can the vendor provide case studies and customer referrals of successful deployments with organizations similar to yours?

The answers here can help you de-risk any new bot protection project you undertake and increase the ROI of your implementation by avoiding known pitfalls with particular vendor implementations. You should always look at other companies' feedback on a product—both positive and negative—when choosing what's right for your business.

Professional Services

Enterprises should not need to rely heavily on services due to a product's complexity or difficulty to operate. Instead, professional services should add incremental value through specialized expertise and sharing best practices for bot protection.

Your bot management solution should come with a team of experts that are there when you need them—from onboarding and deployment to consultations, securing special events, and addressing custom requirements fast. In fact, the right solution will save you money in the long run, both in averted costly bot attacks and employee hours spent mitigating bots.

Most bot management reviews validate that threat research expertise and security operations center (SOC) support are essential to staying ahead of fraudsters' latest tactics while also being responsive to your inquiries 24/7. Look for a vendor that will help your business mitigate persistent business risk and save your teams the time they would otherwise spend manually preventing, managing, and recovering from bot attacks.

FORRESTER AND THE FORRESTER WAVE™ REPORT

Forrester Research, a leading global research and advisory firm, is well-known for its in-depth analysis of technology markets and services. The Forrester Wave™ is one of its most respected evaluation frameworks, providing a rigorous, criteria-based assessment of vendors in specific technology markets. By scoring providers on multiple weighted criteria, the Forrester Wave™ report helps enterprises identify solutions that meet high industry standards and align with their needs.

Each Wave™ report offers a graphical representation of vendor performance, dividing providers into Leaders, Strong Performers, Contenders, and Challengers. Forrester's analysis is based on a meticulous evaluation process that includes a blend of quantitative and qualitative factors, such as:

- **Current Offering**: This includes the solution's technical capabilities, such as detection accuracy, ease of integration, and overall performance in mitigating bot threats. For bot management, the report may examine aspects like real-time analysis, multi-layered detection strategies, and advanced AI/ML capabilities.
- **Strategy**: Forrester assesses a vendor's strategic direction, including its commitment to innovation, product roadmap, and approach to evolving bot threats. This includes the vendor's ability to respond to emerging threats and their commitment to research and development in bot detection technology.
- **Market Presence**: This considers the vendor's overall market reach, including customer base, revenue, and geographic reach. It provides a picture of the vendor's stability, growth trajectory, and influence in the industry.

The Forrester Wave™: Bot Management Software, Q3 2024 highlights the strengths and weaknesses of 11 top vendors, offering valuable insights for enterprises evaluating bot management solutions. By choosing a vendor recognized by Forrester and other industry experts, organizations can be confident they are selecting a provider with proven, trusted technology that has been independently vetted for quality and performance.

Transparent & Predictable Pricing

Straightforward pricing enables you to align within your budget and operational needs. Is the vendor's pricing transparent and predictable, not only at inception but also at renewal? Or is the vendor known for unexpected cost hikes? What is the total cost of ownership?

Keep in mind that more resources are required to support more complex software, and ineffective protection leads to higher fraud costs.

What are the potential long-term savings with a proper solution, and how can those savings allow you to refocus your resources on more strategic projects? Look for a vendor with reasonable pricing for the solution offered. Choose a vendor and solution you are confident will mitigate your risk and vulnerability to fraud and resulting damages.

The right solution will save your business more than it costs in the long run.

Customer Support

When something goes wrong or questions arise, you must be able to trust that your vendor can resolve any issues quickly. Will they provide ongoing support and maintenance for the solution?

What is their response time and track record for addressing customer needs and resolving issues? Do they back that up with clear service-level agreements (SLAs)?

Good indicators here include a high customer retention rate, positive user reviews, and an exceptional NPS (Net Promoter Score). Look for a vendor with easy-to-find customer reviews, proven use cases, a responsive customer support team, and clear SLAs that meet your own SLA objectives.

SOC 2 Compliance

Certifications such as SOC 2 provide a critical layer of trust when selecting a bot management platform. These certifications demonstrate that the vendor adheres to rigorous security, availability, and confidentiality standards, as verified by independent auditors.

A SOC 2-certified provider gives assurance that your data will be handled securely and that the platform meets industry best practices for protecting sensitive information. This is particularly important for businesses managing customer data or operating in regulated industries, where compliance is non-negotiable.

By choosing a certified vendor, you reduce your risk exposure and can confidently align with internal governance and external regulatory requirements.

Choosing the right bot management solution is crucial for effectively mitigating online fraud risks. As we've discussed, the key factors to consider include selecting between best-of-suite and best-of-breed solutions, ensuring comprehensive coverage across all endpoints, ease of implementation and use, performance and accuracy, expertise, peer reviews, and reliable customer support. A thorough evaluation based on these criteria will guide you to a solution that not only addresses your current needs but also adapts to evolving threats, providing long-term protection and peace of mind.

With your bot protection strategy in place, it's time to consider how this solution integrates with your broader security and IT infrastructure. In the next chapter, we will explore the various integration points and strategies to seamlessly incorporate bot management into your existing systems. This will ensure a unified and robust defense mechanism, enhancing your overall cybersecurity posture and operational efficiency.

CHAPTER 10: INTEGRATIONS & ECOSYSTEM COMPATIBILITY

Ensuring seamless integration and ecosystem compatibility is crucial when selecting a bot protection solution for your organization. As businesses increasingly rely on interconnected systems and processes, a disjointed or incompatible solution can lead to inefficiencies, hindering your organization's ability to maximize the benefits of bot protection.

Equally important is choosing a bot protection provider with solid partnerships and a diverse ecosystem. A provider with strong alliances with key technology vendors, cloud platforms, and industry-specific solutions ensures that their protection mechanisms are continuously updated and refined. This interconnected network not only enhances the efficacy of the bot protection but also guarantees that it can easily adapt to your existing infrastructure.

A diverse ecosystem also provides access to a wealth of resources, support, and innovations, allowing your organization to stay ahead of emerging threats and leverage the collective expertise of a robust partner network.

The Importance of Seamless Integration

Having a bot protection solution that is easily integrable with your existing infrastructure is vital for several reasons:

Reduced Complexity: Implementing a bot protection solution can be a complex task. However, when it is designed to integrate smoothly with your organization's existing infrastructure, this complexity can be minimized, allowing your security team to focus on preventive measures and proactive planning.

Operational Efficiency: An effective bot protection solution should work effortlessly with your organization's existing tools and systems, enabling seamless data sharing and collaboration. By streamlining bot defense operations, your team can better monitor and manage threats, ensuring a more robust security posture.

Enhanced Agility: As your organization evolves, it is crucial to have a bot protection solution that can scale and adapt to changing business needs. Seamless integration ensures that new tools and technologies can be incorporated with ease, keeping your security infrastructure agile and robust.

Strategies for Achieving Seamless Integration

To achieve a harmonious and efficient security ecosystem, consider the following strategies for seamless integration in bot protection:

Prioritize Compatibility: When selecting a bot protection solution, ensure that it is compatible with your organization's existing tools and systems. This might involve evaluating solutions based on their support for specific platforms, programming languages, or software packages. Remember that implementing a solution that aligns with your existing infrastructure will save significant time and resources in the long run.

Evaluate APIs and SDKs: APIs (Application Programming Interfaces) and SDKs (Software Development Kits) play a crucial role in enabling seamless integration. They allow your organization's IT team to communicate and work effectively with third-party systems used in bot protection. As you deliberate on potential solutions, examine their APIs and SDKs to ensure that they are well-documented, user-friendly, and meet your organization's needs.

Involve Stakeholders: During the evaluation and selection process, involve key stakeholders from relevant departments, such as IT, security, and business operations. By gaining input from those who will directly interact with or benefit from the bot protection solution, you can ensure alignment with business requirements and easier integration.

Plan for Growth: Ensure that the bot protection solution you select is designed to be scalable, supporting your current and future needs with minimal disruption. This might mean prioritizing solutions that are easily adaptable, offer robust support for additional systems, or can be customized to suit your organization's specific requirements.

Partnerships & Ecosystem

In the dynamic landscape of bot management and online fraud prevention, the significance of robust partnerships and ecosystems cannot be overstated. Partnerships between technology providers facilitate the creation of synergistic solutions that leverage the strengths of each partner. By combining expertise, resources, and technologies, these collaborations can develop more advanced and effective security measures.

For instance, the integration of DataDome's machine learning-driven bot protection with AWS's scalable cloud infrastructure illustrates how partnerships can enhance the overall efficacy of cybersecurity solutions (more on this on page 108). Such alliances ensure that the most cutting-edge and adaptive technologies are employed to safeguard digital assets.

Ensuring Compatibility & Interoperability

A diverse ecosystem of technology partnerships ensures that bot protection solutions are compatible with a wide range of platforms, applications, and services. This compatibility is vital for organizations that operate within complex, multi-vendor environments.

When bot protection solutions are designed to integrate seamlessly with various components of an organization's IT infrastructure, they can provide comprehensive coverage without causing disruptions or requiring extensive modifications. This interoperability reduces the risk of security gaps and enhances the overall resilience of the system.

Access to Continuous Innovation & Support

Technology partnerships often include collaborative research and development efforts, leading to continuous innovation in security solutions. Providers with strong partnerships are better equipped to stay ahead of emerging threats by constantly updating their technologies and methodologies.

Additionally, a rich ecosystem of partners provides access to a wealth of support resources, ensuring that organizations can rely on expert assistance when needed. This ongoing support is crucial for maintaining the effectiveness of bot protection measures and quickly addressing any vulnerabilities that may arise.

CASE STUDY

DATADOME & AMAZON WEB SERVICES PARTNERSHIP

Partnerships between technology providers, such as the collaboration between DataDome and Amazon Web Services (AWS), illustrate how integrating advanced solutions can significantly benefit users.

Many enterprises use AWS for its speed, innovation, and scalability, leveraging services such as Amazon Elastic Compute Cloud (EC2), Amazon CloudFront, and AWS Web Application Firewall (WAF). The AWS WAF provides a first layer of defense, protecting web applications and APIs against common web exploits and bots that may affect availability, compromise security, and consume excessive resources via security rules.

DataDome can be deployed alongside AWS WAF as a complementary application security solution to dynamically block the sophisticated bots responsible for online fraud, like account takeovers, card cracking, fake account creation, payment fraud, and more. Paired together, DataDome and AWS WAF provide the most effective, multi-layered application security available.

DataDome's solution deploys quickly on Amazon CloudFront and integrates with AWS Lambda@Edge, offering real-time protection without the need for additional infrastructure management.

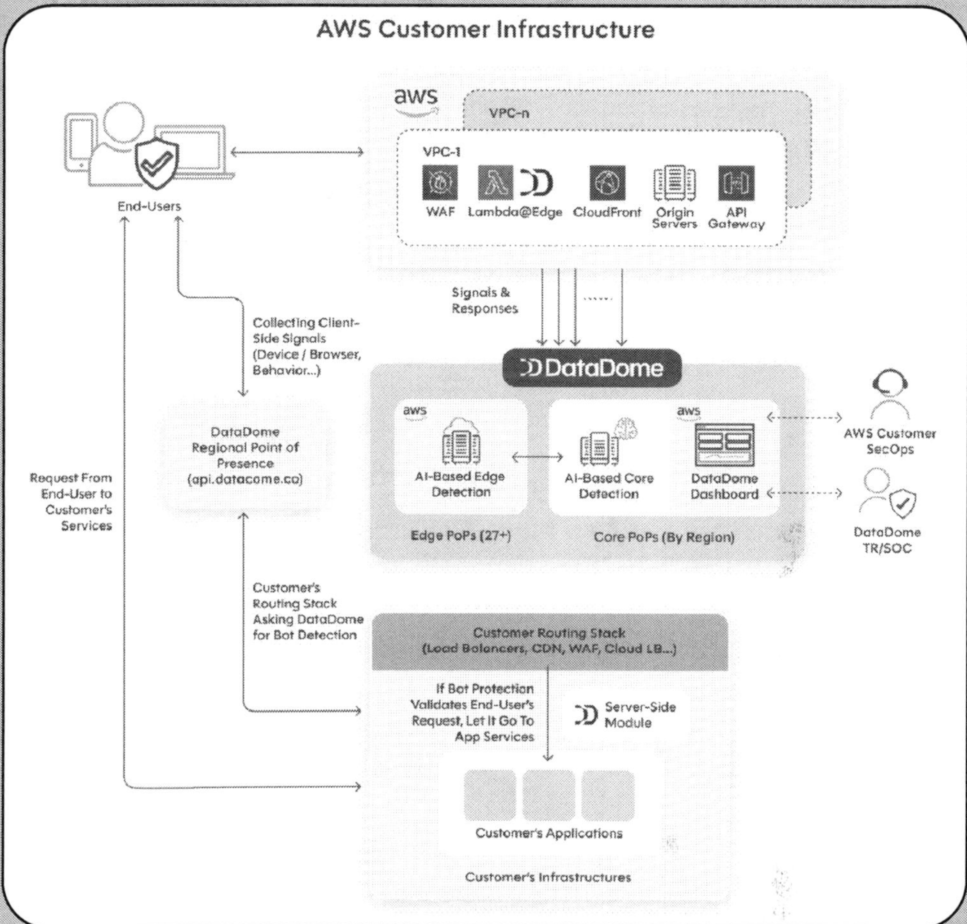

A notable example of the effectiveness of the DataDome and AWS partnership is seen in the case of AMARA. By implementing DataDome's solution, AMARA reduced its server load by 15% and eliminated bot incidents, demonstrating the tangible benefits of this integrated approach to bot management and online fraud prevention.

This partnership showcases how combining the strengths of leading technology providers can deliver robust, scalable, and efficient security solutions, ultimately enhancing user experience and protecting digital assets.

Strategic Advantage & Competitive Edge

Organizations that leverage strong partnerships and a diverse ecosystem gain a strategic advantage. By using best-in-class solutions from leading technology providers, they can offer superior security to their customers, thereby enhancing their reputation and competitiveness in the market. This competitive edge is particularly important in industries where trust and security are key to customer retention and brand loyalty.

In bot management and online fraud prevention, seamless integration and ecosystem compatibility are paramount. Selecting bot protection solutions that integrate effortlessly with existing systems is essential to reduce complexity, enhance operational efficiency, and maintain agility as business needs evolve.

Strategic partnerships play a crucial role in ensuring compatibility, fostering innovation, and providing robust support. Combining expertise from various domains help solution providers stay ahead of emerging threats and protect your digital assets effectively. Adopting solutions that emphasize compatibility will help create a resilient security infrastructure.

CHAPTER 11: PRIVACY CONSIDERATIONS

As the digital landscape evolves, so does the increasingly complex web of laws and regulations designed to protect consumer data and privacy while mitigating fraudulent activities.

Historically, cybersecurity has been focused on protecting endpoints, sometimes to the detriment of the online experience. As more and more businesses are growing their online footprints, security layers are called to respect—if not enhance—the user experience or risk alienating both businesses and their customers. As focus has shifted toward improving the user experience, the privacy of end users' data has not been equally prioritized.

This chapter provides an overview of the key legal and compliance considerations for bot management and online fraud prevention in 2025 and beyond.

Navigating Relevant Laws & Regulations

Privacy is a fundamental human right, one that is increasingly protected by compliance restrictions around the globe, including regulations for data privacy in cybersecurity.

A good bot management solution will make every accommodation to respect your end-users' privacy while also supporting the optimal user experience.

Best practices are to ensure your platform and security solutions are compliant with as many data privacy regulations as possible.

General Data Protection Regulation (GDPR)

The GDPR, implemented by the European Union in 2018, is one of the most stringent data protection laws globally. It emphasizes the protection of personal data and grants individuals significant rights over their data.

Under the GDPR, organizations must collect only the data that is necessary for the specific purpose, a principle known as data minimization. Explicit consent from users is required before any data processing can occur, ensuring that individuals are fully aware of and agree to how their data will be used.

Additionally, individuals have the right to access their data and request its deletion if they choose to do so. In the event of a data breach, organizations are mandated to notify both the authorities and affected individuals within 72 hours.

For bot management, this means implementing robust consent mechanisms for any data collection activities and ensuring that detection methods do not infringe on user privacy. Regular audits of data collection and processing practices are essential to maintain compliance and uphold the standards set by the GDPR.

The Risks of Not Being GDPR Compliant

Navigating the complexities of data protection requires balancing privacy, cybersecurity, and compliance effectively, and understanding the consequences of noncompliance is critical.

General Data Protection Regulation (GDPR) Penalties
Under the GDPR, a violation can lead to fines up to €20 million or 4% of your total annual revenue, whichever is higher. You may also be banned from processing data.

Every country has its own Data Protection Authority (DPA) that determines fines and processing restrictions. In some cases, the DPA may choose to apply both.

Damage of Company Reputation

GDPR violations are public record. News organizations often report on GDPR fines and penalties. The reputational impact can have a ripple effect: customers read about the violation, no longer trust you, and choose a competitor instead.

Cost of Damage Control

Overcoming damage to your reputation also costs money. You may need to pay a public relations firm to help you:

- Respond to media inquiries.
- Monitor the news for articles.
- Communicate the issue on your website.

Liability for Damages

Under Article 82, the GDPR gives data subjects the right to receive compensation for material or non-material damages arising from a violation. If you violate the GDPR, data subjects can file a lawsuit, leading to attorney fees and payment for any assessed damages.

Withdrawal of GDPR Certification

To enable data subjects, some companies achieved a GDPR certification under Article 42 as part of being transparent. A GDPR violation might mean that you no longer meet the certification criteria, enabling certification bodies to revoke it.

California Consumer Privacy Act (CCPA) and California Privacy Rights Act (CPRA)

The CCPA & the CPRA grant California residents enhanced privacy rights and control over their personal information. Businesses that collect personal data from California residents and meet certain criteria are required to comply with this law.

Under these two laws, organizations must disclose the types of data they collect and the purposes for which it is used. Consumers must be provided with an option to opt-out of the sale or sharing of their personal information. They also have the right to access and delete their personal data, and businesses are prohibited from discriminating against consumers who exercise these rights.

In the context of fraud prevention, companies need to develop transparent data collection and usage policies. Fraud prevention measures must be designed to comply with data access and deletion requests, ensuring that consumer rights are respected while maintaining security. Systems should be implemented to facilitate consumer rights under these laws, balancing the need for security with privacy considerations.

Other Relevant Regulations

Beyond the GDPR and CCPA/CPRA, there are several other regulations that impact bot management and fraud prevention. As an example, the ePrivacy Regulation in the EU complements the GDPR with specific rules on electronic communications and tracking technologies.

ARE YOU BETTER PREPARED THAN THESE COMPANIES WERE?[1]

Meta Ireland (2023): Insufficient EU-US data transfer safeguards & processing children's data without parental consent. GDPR fine: € 1.2 billion.

Amazon (2021): Tracking user data without appropriate consent or opt-out options. GDPR fine: € 746 million.

TikTok (2023): Inadequate handling of children's personal data. GDPR fine: € 345 million.

Criteo (2023): Personalized advertising without obtaining valid consent. GDPR fine: € 40 million.

TIM SpA (2023): Personal data from millions of hacked user accounts exposed between 2015 and 2017. GDPR fine: € 7.6 million.

Clearview AI (2024): Unlawful scraping and storing of personal data, including biometric information for facial recognition purposes. GDPR fine: € 30.5 million.[2]

1 https://secureprivacy.ai/blog/gdpr-fines-2023
2 https://www.autoriteitpersoonsgegevens.nl/en/current/dutch-dpa-imposes-a-fine-on-clearview-because-of-illegal-data-collection-for-facial-recognition

Local data privacy regulations also impact bot mitigation's field, for example Singapore's Personal Data Protection Act (PDPA) sets out data protection obligations for organizations operating within the country. Similarly, Brazil's General Data Protection Law (LGPD) regulates the processing of personal data within Brazil.

Each of these regulations adds layers of complexity to the compliance landscape, requiring organizations to stay informed and adaptive to various international standards.

Understanding SOC 2 and Its Role in Compliance & Privacy

SOC 2 (System and Organization Controls 2) certification is a critical benchmark for evaluating how effectively a vendor safeguards sensitive data. Designed around the Trust Service Criteria—security, availability, processing integrity, confidentiality, and privacy—SOC 2 demonstrates that an organization has implemented robust controls to manage and protect customer data. It is an independent validation that a vendor adheres to industry best practices, making it an essential consideration for businesses managing sensitive customer information.

Why SOC 2 Matters for Compliance and Privacy

SOC 2 compliance is particularly important for businesses operating in regulated industries such as finance, healthcare, and e-commerce, where data breaches and compliance violations can lead to severe legal and reputational consequences. A SOC 2-certified vendor offers assurance that their systems and processes are designed to meet stringent security and privacy requirements, ensuring alignment with regulatory frameworks like GDPR, CCPA, and HIPAA.

For privacy management, SOC 2 certification provides a structured framework to handle sensitive data responsibly. This reduces the risk of breaches and simplifies compliance with internal and external audits, giving organizations confidence in their privacy protocols while building trust with their customers.

SOC 2 vs. SOC 2 Type 2: A Key Differentiator

When evaluating a vendor, it's crucial to understand whether their certification is SOC 2 or SOC 2 Type 2:

- SOC 2 assesses whether appropriate controls are in place as of a specific point in time.
- SOC 2 Type 2, considered the gold standard, evaluates the effectiveness of those controls over an extended period, demonstrating sustained reliability and operational maturity.

For businesses seeking to ensure continuous data protection, SOC 2 Type 2 certification offers stronger assurance that the vendor's controls are consistently operating as intended.

How to Assess a Vendor's SOC 2 Certification

To verify SOC 2 compliance:

- Ask vendors for their SOC 2 audit report, which details the scope, criteria, and findings of their certification process.
- Prioritize vendors with SOC 2 Type 2 certification.
- Look for any exceptions or weaknesses noted in the audit report and ensure the vendor has addressed them adequately.

By choosing a SOC 2-certified vendor, businesses not only meet regulatory requirements but also strengthen their overall data security posture.

This chapter has provided an overview of the critical legal and compliance considerations for bot management and online fraud prevention. By following the guidelines and best practices outlined, you can ensure that your organization remains compliant and effectively safeguards users' data and privacy.

CHAPTER 12: FUTURE TRENDS & EMERGING TRENDS

The landscape of bot management and online fraud prevention continues to undergo significant transformations. The ongoing evolution of technology continues to shape both the methods of attack and the strategies for defense.

In this chapter, we will explore some of the current trends and emerging threats that will define the next era of bot management.

Puppeteer Extra Stealth is Dead—Long Live Anti-CDP Bot Frameworks

When it comes to bot development, it's difficult not to mention Puppeteer Extra Stealth, one of the most popular anti-detect bot frameworks. It offers bot developers several features to lie about a bot's fingerprint and is even integrated with CAPTCHA farms.

Lately, however, Puppeteer Extra Stealth's popularity is declining. No significant code change or update has been pushed within the last year, and the primary code maintainer started his own paid bot product.

But that's not the only reason to explain the decrease of popularity. Indeed, the latest update of Headless Chrome makes automated browsers more difficult to detect by default. With just a few changes, there are very few inconsistencies left in the fingerprint of Headless Chrome.

The lack of maintenance of Puppeteer Extra Stealth, combined with the major Headless Chrome update and new CDP detection techniques, led the bot dev community to create new anti-detect bot frameworks. These new frameworks include nodriver (announced as the successor of undetected chromedriver), and Selenium driverless. To avoid being detected, these frameworks decided not to rely on Chromedriver and Selenium. Instead, they implement all the usual bot automation functions using low-level CDP commands that do not leverage Runtime.enable.

Even though these frameworks are quite new, they are already popular.

It's Not Just About Automated (Headless) Browsers

It has become easier to forge all kinds of signals, including low-level signals that used to be difficult to forge consistently.

For example, the Noble TLS library enables bot developers to replace their usual Python HTTP client with an HTTP client that has a consistent TLS fingerprint.

Developers just need to provide a user-agent, e.g. Mozilla/5.0 (Macintosh; Intel Mac OS X 10_15_7) AppleWebKit/537.36 (KHTML, like Gecko) Chrome/125.0.0.0 Safari/537.36 for Chrome 125 on MacOS, and the library takes care of updating the TLS fingerprint accordingly. This is particularly useful for attackers to bypass server-side-only detection mechanisms and static signatures/rules implemented in WAFs.

Besides forging fingerprinting signals, several libraries—such as Ghost cursor—help bots generate more realistic and human-like mouse movements.

Instead of moving the mouse in a straight line, it helps users to generate mouse movements with a less suspicious trajectory using Bezier curves.

Ghost cursor is also compatible with Puppeteer, one of the most popular bot automation frameworks. Thus, bot developers don't need to modify all of their code to benefit from this library.

Bots as a Service: Proxy Networks Make the Lives of Bot Developers Easier

Lately, most of the popular proxy networks started to provide scraping bots as a service. Bot as a service (BaaS) providers let users run bots at scale without requiring any bot development or reverse engineering knowledge.

A BaaS is simply a REST API on which a user provides the URL they want to scrape. The business model is simple: users only pay when their request is successful. Therefore, as long as the request is blocked, the user doesn't pay for anything. No need to worry about proxy bandwidth, which can become expensive when using residential proxies.

If the request is blocked, the BaaS will make several requests in parallel in an attempt to bypass the protection. For example, they may:

- Rotate user agent.
- Spoof new HTTP headers.
- Change IP address by using new proxies.
- Forge a CAPTCHA.

How Bots as a Service (BaaS) Works

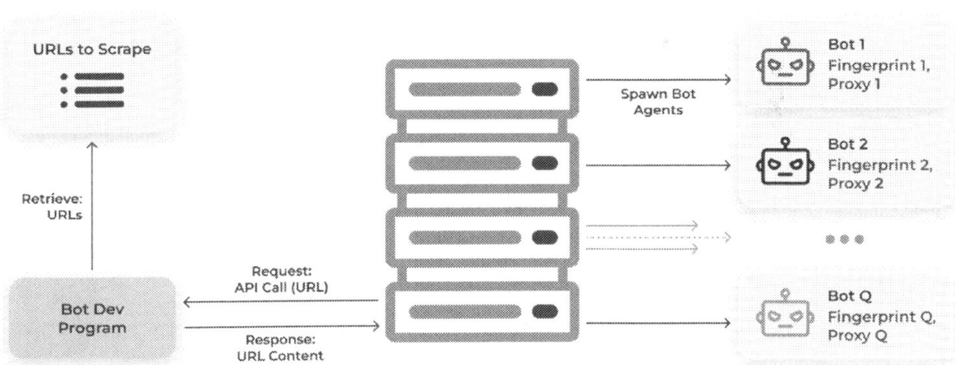

If at some point, the BaaS is able to get the content without being blocked, it will return the content to the user. The user only pays for a single API call, even though the BaaS had to do dozens of requests to successfully get the content of the page.

OpenBullet Makes Bot Attacks Accessible to Anyone

OpenBullet is an automation suite intended to be used for scraping and parsing data, automated security assessment, and much more. It is used by bot developers to perform automated attacks such as credential stuffing. OpenBullet is released under an open source MIT license on Github.

It does not require programming knowledge to perform simple actions, which makes it uncomplicated to install and use. Several different configurations—sequences of actions to perform activity (such as scraping) on a website—can be found online. Therefore, OpenBullet is typically used by people who want to create bots but lack strong programming knowledge.

Some fraudsters that use OpenBullet prefer it because its configurations can be exported and shared freely. Several forums publish configurations for credential stuffing or scraping online, and some of the most advanced configurations are even for sale. In fact, ready-to-use configurations are easier to find than guides on how to use the software, which could indicate that most OpenBullet users do not have advanced knowledge of the software and depend on others' work to scrape websites.

The big difference from other types of testing suites or automation frameworks is in the ease of use. Everything can be done in visual mode in OpenBullet—meaning there's a simple UI to work with, rather than lines of code. This appeals to people who would otherwise be limited by their programming knowledge. Nevertheless, OpenBullet also provides a high-level programming language that can be used to fine-tune some operations.

The simple UI helps non-programmers build automations for all kinds of web attacks, such as scraping and credential stuffing. Anyone who wants to perform an attack can likely find a configuration that works for their purposes. And even the most simple configurations include a tool to solve traditional CAPTCHAs, as well as integrations with CAPTCHA farms.

While it can be detected by most anti-bot vendors, it should not be underestimated—OpenBullet's ease of use and free ready-to-use attack configurations make it an attractive choice for supporting malicious activity on less-protected websites.

Traditional CAPTCHAs are Definitely Out of the League

Security researchers have shown that traditional CAPTCHAs that rely mostly on the difficulty of their challenge for security have become straightforward to solve using audio and image recognition techniques.

In the past, CAPTCHA farm services such as 2captcha used to rely on human workers from developing countries to solve CAPTCHA on the behalf of bots. With the recent progress in audio and image recognition techniques, new services such as CapSolver were able to both reduce the cost and the price of solving CAPTCHA.

In 2018, it used to cost around $3 to solve 1,000 reCAPTCHA v2 challenges and it took around 45s per reCAPTCHA. Now, CAPTCHA solving services can solve 1,000 reCAPTCHA v2 challenges for $0.8 and 5x less time spent per challenge.

Prompt Injection & Denial of Wallet Attacks

We have previously discussed how generative AI platforms like ChatGPT can cause problems for other websites with their bot usage. As AI apps have grown in popularity and sophistication, however, they have also become targets for malicious actors.

Generative AI systems train on large volumes of data to provide their responses—and they train on the user inputs as well. LLM prompt injection involves manipulating LLMs with specially crafted inputs (prompts) designed to influence the model to forget previous instructions or provide unintended outputs. This can lead to the spread of misinformation, unauthorized access to sensitive data, and financial loss.

Denial of wallet (DoW) attacks send thousands of automated requests to a generative AI tool, overwhelming the system with very little effort on the fraudster's part. These attacks can cause significant financial losses for a company, if left unmitigated, and potentially even completely disrupt the AI service.

Breaking Down The Silos Between Fraud & Cybersecurity Teams

Stopping online fraud can be an overwhelming task due to the continual, increasing, and sophisticated nature of attacks. Fraudsters constantly adapt their methods, making it challenging for businesses to stay ahead.

The traditional separation between cybersecurity and fraud teams is increasingly unsustainable. As Gartner® notes in their 2024 Emerging Tech: Security — Cyber-Fraud Fusion Is the Future of Online Fraud Detection report, "fraudsters don't operate in silos, they don't discriminate when it comes to the tools or tactics utilized; it's all about effectiveness, and they will look across the entire technical landscape for vulnerabilities and opportunities. Fraud has tended to focus on point-in-time solutions, focused on specific use cases. However, the problem is much larger than that; a more comprehensive and holistic approach (that connects isolated teams and systems) is required."[1]

Current fraud mitigation tools are often manual, complex, and reactive, making it difficult to scale for the sheer volume of continual fraud threats. This reactive approach requires an army of fraud managers or auditors to process suspicious and potentially fraudulent transactions. Challenges with these traditional tools include:

- **Manual Processes**: Labor-intensive and slow, unable to keep up with the speed of automated attacks.
- **Complex Systems**: Difficult to integrate with existing IT infrastructure, leading to inefficiencies.
- **Reactive Nature**: Addressing fraud after it occurs rather than preventing it from happening.

Fraud prevention costs are rising due to higher infrastructure and security team resource requirements. Businesses need to invest in more advanced technologies and skilled personnel to combat sophisticated fraud attempts, and realize that bot attacks are a shared problem.

1 Gartner, Emerging Tech: Security – Cyber-Fraud Fusion Is the Future of Online Fraud Detection, Dan Ayoub, Pete Redshaw, 7 September 2023

This core insight has given rise to a new approach—Cyberfraud Prevention & Protection—representing the convergence of cybersecurity and fraud teams into a unified force. According to Gartner®, "by 2028, 20% of large enterprises are expected to adopt cyber-fraud fusion teams, up from less than 5% today."[2]

In many organizations, silos between cybersecurity and fraud teams create protection gaps and opportunities for exploitation. These silos hamper responses because the different teams often have vastly different drivers, tools, metrics, and risk profiles.

The Convergence of Cybersecurity and Fraud Mitigation

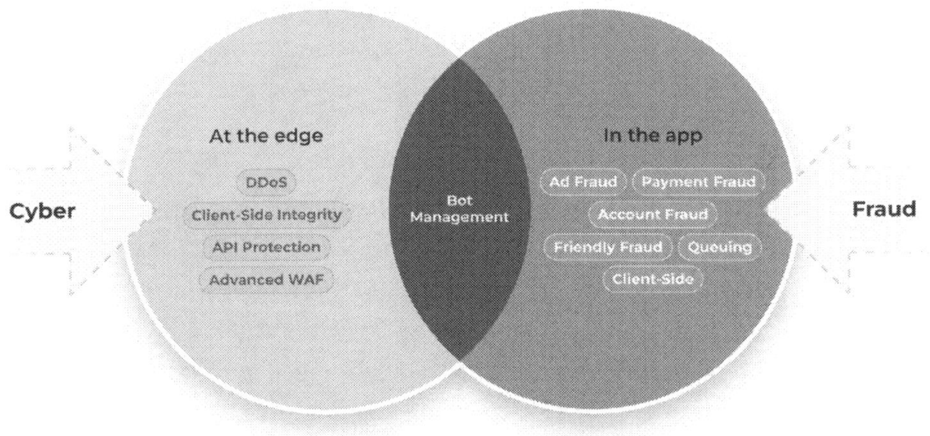

Cybersecurity teams are focused on protecting the IT infrastructure, and fraud mitigation teams are concerned with preventing financial losses. This disconnect can lead to incomplete protection strategies, leaving vulnerabilities that fraudsters can exploit.

While this separation may have made sense in the past, it now leads to several key challenges:

- **Lack of Integrated Threat Intelligence**: Siloed teams miss critical insights by not sharing data across the attack lifecycle. Leveraging downstream behaviors can enhance upstream threat detection.
- **Inefficient Resource Use**: Redundant efforts, tool sprawl, and siloed operations increase costs and slow response times. Often, entire fraud

2 Gartner, Emerging Tech: Security – Cyber-Fraud Fusion Is the Future of Online Fraud Detection, Dan Ayoub, Pete Redshaw, 7 September 2023

teams exist because earlier cyber actions weren't taken.

- **Inconsistent Defense Strategies**: Misaligned defense approaches can create protection gaps. For example, while one team may block credential stuffing, the other may be unaware of related account takeover attempts.

The Emerging Need for Integration

Organizations are beginning to merge the teams, tools, and processes that are used by cybersecurity and fraud prevention teams, respectively. This strategic shift aims to break down operational silos and create a more comprehensive approach to combating online fraud. The fusion of cybersecurity and fraud prevention, termed "cyberfraud fusion" by Gartner, represents a modern and strategic new direction for traditionally separate cybersecurity and fraud detection teams.

The Cyber Fraud Kill Chain & Fusion Centers

The Cyber-Fraud Kill Chain is another key component of this new Cyberfraud paradigm. As Gartner® highlights in their Emerging Tech: Security — Cyber-Fraud Fusion Is the Future of Online Fraud Detection report, "The cyber-fraud kill chain has emerged as a form of "fraud intelligence." It combines common methodologies widely used within cybersecurity to profile the tools, tactics, and procedures (TTPs) of adversaries by creating a holistic framework from which policies and rules can be added to fraud prevention platforms."[3]

Bridging the Gap: A Unified Approach

To combat cyberfraud threats, organizations need to foster better collaboration between cybersecurity and fraud mitigation teams. This can be achieved through:

- **Integrated Tools and Platforms**: Utilizing tools that provide a holistic view of threats across both cybersecurity and fraud domains.
- **Cross-Functional Training**: Ensuring both teams understand the other's challenges and methodologies.
- **Unified Metrics and Goals**: Establishing common metrics and goals that align the objectives of both teams.

---

3 Gartner, Emerging Tech: Security – Cyber-Fraud Fusion Is the Future of Online Fraud Detection, Dan Ayoub, Pete Redshaw, 7 September 2023

CASE STUDY

CASE STUDY: APPLYING CYBER PRINCIPLES TO COMBATTING ORGANIZED RETAIL CRIME

Target's strategy to address organized retail crime (ORC) exemplifies the importance of collaboration between cybersecurity and fraud prevention teams. ORC has evolved, with criminals increasingly using digital tools to carry out complex schemes that affect both online and physical retail operations. Recognizing this shift, Target has moved toward an integrated approach, where cybersecurity, fraud prevention, and asset protection teams work together.[1]

This collaboration allows for real-time sharing of threat intelligence, enabling the development of sophisticated tools that adapt to the ever-changing tactics of criminals. For example, Target's teams jointly analyze data from various sources, allowing them to spot patterns and vulnerabilities that might be missed if each team worked independently. This integrated effort not only improves the detection and prevention of fraud but also enhances the customer experience by ensuring that security measures do not interfere with legitimate transactions.

Moreover, the partnership between these teams has led to more proactive strategies, where potential threats are identified and mitigated before they can cause significant harm. This approach has proven effective in protecting Target's assets and customers, demonstrating that collaboration across traditionally separate domains is crucial in addressing the complexities of modern retail crime.

In summary, Target's success in fighting ORC underscores the need for retail companies to foster close cooperation between their cybersecurity, fraud prevention, and asset protection teams to stay ahead of increasingly sophisticated criminal networks.

---

1 https://tech.target.com/blog/cybersecurity-combatting-organized-retail-crime

To effectively combat online fraud, it is crucial to anticipate the visitor's intention. A robust defense starts with understanding the behavior of potential fraudsters, allowing businesses to block malicious activity before it can cause harm.

By establishing intent and behavior earlier, businesses can prevent fraud before it happens, rather than reacting to it post-incident. Essentially, this means putting the vault door at the front door, making access harder from the start, and blocking bots before they can infiltrate and cause damage.

CONCLUSION

The evolution of bots over the past decade has been nothing short of remarkable. From simple scripts to advanced automation, bots have become more than just a disruptive force—they are now integral to a wide range of malicious activities, from scraping to account takeovers and payment fraud.

In the last 12 months, we've seen even basic bots adopt advanced techniques like fingerprinting evasion, human-like interaction simulation, and the manipulation of network signals. These advancements have made detecting and mitigating bot attacks increasingly difficult, particularly for companies still relying on traditional defenses.

With the rise of Bots as a Service (BaaS), deploying sophisticated bot attacks is easier than ever, meaning even non-technical actors can initiate attacks at scale. Fraudsters now have access to tools that can mimic legitimate user behavior, bypass IP-based defenses, and evade detection with alarming accuracy.

This rapid evolution presents a critical challenge to businesses, making it clear that traditional security measures are no longer enough to protect against the increasingly advanced tactics used by bots today.

What Experts and Advanced Tools Are Doing to Help Solve the Problem

As bots become more sophisticated, so too must the solutions designed to combat them. At the forefront of this battle is machine learning (ML), which has proven to be one of the most effective tools for identifying and blocking malicious bot activity.

DataDome's platform, for example, leverages advanced fingerprinting techniques, ML-based behavioral analysis, and real-time monitoring to detect and block both simple and complex bots. By analyzing trillions of signals daily, these solutions can distinguish between legitimate users and bots with greater precision than ever before, helping businesses protect their digital assets without introducing friction to real customers.

Moreover, innovation in fraud detection is happening across industries. The use of advanced frameworks, anti-detection techniques, and AI has made it possible for security systems to stay ahead of attackers.

The more data and attack patterns these systems process, the more accurate and proactive they become in neutralizing threats. This continual evolution is key to combating the rising tide of bot-driven attacks.

Agentic AI: The New Challenge in Distinguishing Good vs. Bad Bots

The rise of Agentic AI—AI-powered programs that autonomously perceive, decide, and act—is blurring the lines between legitimate automation and malicious bot activity. Unlike traditional bots that follow scripts, these AI-driven agents can navigate websites like humans, adapt to security measures, and execute fraud with unprecedented sophistication. Businesses are already seeing AI agents used for both beneficial tasks, like content discovery and automation, and harmful activities, such as scraping, credential stuffing, and payment fraud.

As AI-driven threats grow, bot detection must evolve beyond simple human vs. bot classification to distinguish between legitimate vs. illegitimate AI agents in real time. Businesses will need AI-powered detection that leverages behavioral analysis, machine learning at the edge, and advanced fingerprinting to accurately differentiate between AI-driven fraud and trusted automation—ensuring security without blocking beneficial agentic interactions.

Cyberfraud Protection: The Convergence of Fraud and Cybersecurity Teams

One of the most promising developments in the fight against bots is the convergence of fraud and cybersecurity teams. Traditionally, these two functions operated in silos, but as bot attacks increasingly straddle the lines between fraud and cybersecurity, collaboration has become essential. By sharing data, insights, and tools, fraud and security teams can create a more holistic defense strategy that addresses both automated and manual threats.

This integrated approach allows businesses to better understand the full scope of threats they face and respond more quickly to attacks. For instance, intelligence gathered from fraud detection systems can inform cybersecurity protocols, making the entire security framework more robust. The convergence of these teams will be crucial as businesses strive to defend themselves against the increasingly complex nature of online threats.

Stopping fraud before it happens is one of the most powerful ways to curb bot activity. When fraud becomes harder to commit, it not only frustrates fraudsters but also deters them from deploying bots in the first place. Bots are often used as tools for scaling fraud—whether it's account takeovers, payment fraud, or scraping sensitive information—but when these automated attacks consistently fail, the incentive to use bots diminishes.

By strengthening your defenses against fraud through advanced machine learning, behavioral analysis, and continuous monitoring, you're not just reacting to attacks—you're cutting them off at the source. This preemptive approach is key because when fraud becomes less profitable and more difficult to execute, the entire ecosystem of bot-driven fraud is undermined. In turn, the threat of bots becomes less prevalent, making your business more secure in the long run.

Looking to the Future

As bots grow more sophisticated, the need for businesses to stay ahead of these threats has never been more urgent. The insights shared in this book have hopefully given you a deeper understanding of the complexities surrounding bot attacks and the tools available to defend against them. By leveraging advanced technologies like AI, integrating fraud and cybersecurity efforts, and taking proactive tactical steps, businesses can not only protect their operations but also create a safer, more resilient digital environment for the future.

The fight against bots is ongoing, but by working together, sharing knowledge, and staying vigilant, we can overcome these challenges. Let's continue to evolve our defenses, adapt to new threats, and build a more secure digital world—together.

ABOUT THE AUTHOR

Benjamin Fabre is the technical co-founder and CEO of DataDome, an industry-leading AI-powered platform that protects global enterprises from cyberfraud and sophisticated bot-driven attacks. With nearly 20 years of expertise in scalable cloud infrastructure, machine learning, and SaaS technologies, Benjamin has built his career pioneering solutions that defend against evolving online threats.

As true cybersecurity visionaries, the DataDome founding team anticipated the surge of bot-driven fraud and recognized the need for an instantaneous response at the edge. Understanding that static rules would always lag behind, they embarked on a mission to build a transparent and user-friendly anti-bot solution.

Under Benjamin's leadership, DataDome has consistently been recognized as a leader in its field. The platform was named a Leader in The Forrester Wave™: Bot Management Software Q3 2024 report, is consistently ranked as a G2 Leader, and was honored as one of G2's Best Security Products of 2024. The company was also recognized as one of Viva Technology's 2024 Next 100 Unicorns, and has repeatedly placed on both the Inc. 500 and Deloitte Technology Fast 500 lists.

Before co-founding DataDome, Benjamin co-founded and led a social media monitoring & data analysis platform to a successful exit. He is also an active member of the Forbes Technology Council, Co-President of La French Tech New York, is a Partner at 50 Partners, and is an investor at ISAI & Irregular Expression.

Made in the USA
Columbia, SC
06 July 2025

60382765R00076